DEAR *Next* PRIME MINISTER

DEAR *Next* PRIME MINISTER

OPEN LETTERS TO MARGARET THATCHER & NEIL KINNOCK

EDITED BY NEIL ASTLEY

BLOODAXE BOOKS

Copyright © Bloodaxe Books Ltd 1990.
Copyright of letters resides with authors as listed.

ISBN: 1 85224 151 9

First published 1990 by
Bloodaxe Books Ltd,
P.O. Box 1SN,
Newcastle upon Tyne NE99 1SN.

Bloodaxe Books Ltd acknowledges
the financial assistance of Northern Arts.

Typesetting by EMS Phototypesetting, Berwick upon Tweed.

Printed in Great Britain by
Billing & Sons Limited, Worcester.

CONTENTS

Denis Healey   *1*

Kenneth Baker   *4*

William Rodgers   *7*

David Icke   *11*

Bryan Gould   *15*

David Blunkett   *18*

Alan Plater   *21*

Lisa Appignanesi   *23*

John J. Vincent   *25*

Daniel Easterman   *30*

Sheila Kitzinger   *33*

Lucy Ellmann   *35*

Jo Richardson   *37*

Michèle Roberts   *40*

Sue Slipman   *42*

Brenda Dean   *45*

Marina Warner   *48*

Ben Pimlott   *50*

David Constantine   *54*

Penelope Fitzgerald   *57*

Hans Eysenck   *60*

Paul Davies   *65*

Sir Roy Shaw   *68*

Timothy Waterstone   *71*

John Calder   *74*

Tessa Blackstone   *76*

Vivien Stern   *79*

Julian Mitchell   *82*

Jeanette Winterson   *85*

Margaret Drabble   *87*

David Astor   *90*

Richard Mabey   *93*

Ted Hughes   *96*

John May/David Powell   *97*

Tam Dalyell   *100*

Ann Clwyd   *103*

Peter Hain   *107*

Jan Morris   *110*

Anne Smith   *113*

Ian Paisley   *116*

Fintan O'Toole   *119*

Bruce Kent   *122*

Norris McWhirter   *125*

Paul Oestreicher   *128*

Ron Todd   *131*

Brian Aldiss   *134*

H. R. F. Keating   *137*

Chad Varah   *139*

Leo Abse   *142*

D. M. Thomas   *145*

Michael Blackburn   *147*

Peter Levi   *149*

Auberon Waugh   *151*

Christopher Logue   *152*

Stan Barstow   *152*

Elizabeth Wilson   *154*

Henry Livings   *157*

Jonathan Raban   *158*

Doris Lessing   *161*

Colin Wilson   *162*

Ken Loach, John Lister
& Alan Thornett   *168*

Arnold Wesker   *171*

Michael Winner   *177*

Peter Barnes   *179*

FOREWORD

Dear Mrs Thatcher, Dear Mr Kinnock,

I expect you spend most of your time with close colleagues, friends and party supporters. There can't be many opportunities for other people to grab your attention and tell you what they think of your policies.

In judging public reaction to those policies, you can't rely just on what you read in the press or hear on radio and television, for politics has to be packaged by the media in restrictive formats. You'll be asked to defend one of your policies, and then your opponent is called upon to disagree with you. An extremist is grilled about his unacceptable actions, and then a minister tries to excuse his unacceptable methods of dealing with the extremist. An opposition spokesman condemns the extremist and the minister. A commentator draws parallels, delivers further opinions, and then gives a summary which is really an interpretation.

In trying to create a balanced presentation of political issues, there is a danger of oversimplification, of reinforcing the public's perception of politics as antagonistic, as being about irreconcilable opposites or mutually exclusive two-party alternatives. Conflict makes good copy; disagreement makes good television.

This media packaging is designed to make events fit into these kinds of moulds, but the issues themselves are never black and white, never red and blue. Complex issues are often reduced to one-line replies, sound-bites and summings-up. A discussion or debate turns into an argument or slanging-match in which no one can put over a point of view without being derided or shouted down. There's never enough time: 'I'm sorry, I'll have to cut you off there...We've just time for a quick reaction from...How would you sum that up?...I'll have to stop you there...'

If this is how the public is fed its politics, it's no wonder that they're fed up with it all. Party political broadcasts too have been turned into guileful exercises in people manipulation, yet few people can be so gullible as to be taken in by this. Credibility is not a matter of image, or saying the right thing, it's to do with trust and respect: not just whether you believe someone, but whether they themselves believe what they're saying.

Our electoral system gives voters a "choice" of two extremes, but I don't believe people want a government whose policies are dictated by ideology, they want one which addresses human issues in human terms. Ideology has been discredited in Eastern Europe, but people power has still to make its mark in British politics. You, Mrs Thatcher, are becoming more and more isolated from the people. You, Mr Kinnock, are trying too hard to find the common touch. I can't be alone in thinking that you'd both have much to gain from listening to other people's views, and not just to advisors, colleagues and commentators.

This book of letters gives you the chance to listen to some other opinions. We had the idea of asking a number of leading writers, campaigners and political experts to imagine what they would say to you about your policies if they were closeted with you for five minutes.

I had expected that many would want to write to you about the environment, but the single most pressing issue turned out to be education. Given people's concern about the future and their children's future, perhaps this wasn't so surprising. Ted Hughes wrote about the environment *and* education. Other writers took up related areas such as childcare, science and the arts.

You may be obsessed with the economy, but this wasn't a passion shared by our contributors. The reasons for this may well lie behind Arnold Wesker's view that controlling the economy (or good house-keeping, as you've called it, Mrs Thatcher) isn't the first priority in most people's minds: 'House-keeping is the least we expect of government.' You will decide our budget, whether we like it or not, but what is important to us is not how we manage that budget but how we live our lives.

In a book of this kind, there are bound to be gaps. It cannot be fully comprehensive, but we've tried to make it as representative as possible, and where gaps became apparent during its compilation, we did try to redress them by soliciting letters from people concerned with those issues. However, we had to admit defeat in some areas: we asked many people for letters about Europe, immigration and black issues, but they either didn't have the time or weren't interested in contributing to the book.

Similarly, Labour MPs and front bench spokesmen were eager to publicise their views in a book representing a wide spectrum of political opinion, but their Conservative counterparts were most reluctant bedfellows. Apart from Kenneth Baker, most were either 'too busy' or not willing to be associated with a book of this kind.

This pattern was repeated amongst the writers. While D. M. Thomas was willing not only to sing your praises, Mrs Thatcher, but to have a swipe at 'deckchair socialists', others were almost coy in demurring to oblige. A. N. Wilson said: 'How could one cram into one thousand words all the things one might have to say to the Prime

Minister?' Michael Oakeshott claimed: 'I would have nothing interesting to say.' Pressure of work prevented Roger Scruton from contributing, but his reaction says a lot about how you, Mr Kinnock, are viewed by many right-wing intellectuals: 'Neil Kinnock says nothing with which I can either agree or disagree since he seems to me to say nothing (or, alternatively, everything, which is the same thing).'

There was a reluctance of another kind on the part of centre party politicians and supporters. Alan Beith said: 'I find the format of the proposed book particularly unattractive in that it seems to assume a two-party political system in which Mrs Thatcher and Mr Kinnock are the only appropriate recipients of political ideas.' Sir Peter Parker liked the idea of the book, but regretted 'that you have to accept the inevitable two-party line of the future. There is a need to remind both leaders that there is every chance at the next election that the 15-20% of us (who are determined on some constitutional reform) might be able to force the pace on a fairer system of representation.'

Paddy Ashdown wouldn't contribute a letter because 'I do not think that this would be an appropriate thing for me to do.' I'm especially grateful to William Rodgers and David Icke that they did feel it appropriate to write you a letter for public consumption. One thing this book does show – and Stan Barstow takes this up directly in his letter – is that there is considerable support in Britain for proportional representation. Many of your own voters would like to see consensus government, and agree with the Liberal Democrats that this will only be achieved through electoral reform. If you, Mr Kinnock, were to add a wholehearted commitment to proportional representation to your new manifesto, I cannot see how you could fail to become the next Prime Minister.

Petra Kelly was rushing round Eastern Europe when we caught up with her, but she did manage to dash off a telegram: 'I would tell Mrs Thatcher to visit children's cancer wards, spend a week in the dying forests of Eastern Europe, take a trip on the Rainbow Warrior of Greenpeace, repair the damaged medieval statues on the Cologne Dome, visit the Indian tribes in the Amazonas, and watch wood chipping companies cutting down rainforest. She might then realise that the Earth has no emergency exit and that we are living in an age of environmental crises. This is the time for radical environmental protection – if there is a future, it will be green!'

Can we hope for a green future under your governments? Perhaps we may if you're willing to take note of these letters. A repeated criticism made of you, Mrs Thatcher, is that you don't listen to other people, while you, Mr Kinnock, are accused of a lack of intellectual rigour. I would like to think that it's at least possible for this book to shake those stereotypes.

Many people despair of politics because they see politicians as unresponsive and only concerned with defending their own entrenched positions. Others feel disenfranchised by what they see as a lack of choice. That's why they were attracted to the *idea* of the SDP, and why they will continue to vote for parties who have no hope of gaining power under our present electoral system.

Ken Russell's response to the book was typical: 'In my opinion your idea is a sheer waste of time and effort. The messages in the book will fall on deaf ears. I'm of the opinion that politics is the last refuge of the scoundrel.' I'd like to think we can prove him wrong.

Ralph Steadman wouldn't give you the benefit of his attention: 'They get far too much already. Indifference towards them would be far better medicine. We encourage politicians by paying them so much lip service. Personally, I won't even draw them any more.' Alasdair Gray was of a similar opinion: 'Imagining speaking to Kinnock or Thatcher gives me a sensation of such mind-blasting futility that I can't even pretend to do it.'

Dear Mrs Thatcher, Will you listen to the people who have wanted to speak to you through this book? Dear Mr Kinnock, Will you think about what they have to say? As for the book itself: if you don't have time to read it right through, you can at least read it in snatches, one letter at a time. We hope you'll take it in the spirit of Alan Plater's letter and regard it as 'a friendly contribution to the free flow of ideas vital to the health and humour of a civilised democracy'.

Yours sincerely,

NEIL ASTLEY,
Editor.

Neil Astley is the editor and managing director of Bloodaxe Books. He worked as a journalist for four years before reading English at Newcastle University, and founded Bloodaxe Books in 1978. In 1982 he received an Eric Gregory Award for his poetry from the Society of Authors. His first book of poems, *Darwin Survivor* (Peterloo Poets, 1988), is a Poetry Book Society Recommendation, and his anthologies include the Bloodaxe "sampler" *Poetry with an Edge*.

DENIS HEALEY

House of Commons,
London SW1.

Dear Prime Minister,

'There is no such thing as society, there are only individuals and families.' That statement of your faith explains why you could describe people who talk of social responsibility as 'drooling and drivelling about caring'.

What does puzzle me a little, however, is that, while rejecting society, you nevertheless believe that there is such a thing as the State, quite irrespective of individuals and their families. Moreover you believe that the nation state is something which can and must possess absolute sovereignty. Jingoism is the hallmark of your foreign policy.

As a result, Thatcherism has come to resemble Communism as a political ideology which asserts values wholly independent of the real attitudes of those individuals and families it purports to represent; in Professor Talmon's phrase, it is a species of 'totalitarian democracy'.

You see all forms of independent social organisation as necessarily hostile to the State – as 'the enemy within'. The trade unions and local government were your first targets. Since then you have turned your attention to the BBC, the press, the universities, the House of Lords, the House of Commons and even to the monarchy. Even the legal and medical professions, traditionally your Party's most loyal supporters, have not escaped your censure. I sometimes think that if you had your way, the only British institutions which remained intact would be MI5 and the SAS. Your motto is *'l'état c'est moi'*.

Yet democracy cannot survive unless a multiplicity of non-governmental organisations can provide it with social tissue. By trying to undermine them, you undermine democracy itself. A free people is not just an aggregate of individuals and their families. It is also a collection of communities organised to support the common interests which they reflect. For you, such communities are necessarily hostile to the state. Indeed you see consensus as a dirty word, used only by 'quislings and traitors', as you told Tony Parsons.

Most individuals believe, however vaguely, in human brotherhood and see consensus as a step towards it. They think the state should accept the same view. You, however, believe that the state should have no social responsibilities, and should hand them over, with all its economic responsibilities except the control of inflation, to market forces.

Your academic acolytes attribute your ideology to Adam Smith. But Adam Smith insisted that the market could never provide the economic and social infrastructure on which private industry depends. He said that the state must ensure the provision of necessities, which he defined as 'whatever the custom of the country renders it indecent for creditable people, even of the lowest order, to be without'. Thus he rejected the Poll Tax not only because it was inefficient but also because it was bound to be 'either altogether arbitrary or altogether unequal'.

By attempting to adhere instead to the comic-strip economics of the sado-monetarists you have produced exactly the opposite of what you promised. Inflation was to be 'the judge and jury' of your success. It is now higher in Britain than in any other major industrial country. Production and productivity are lower. We have the largest trade deficit and the highest interest rates in the industrial world. Both the state and individuals are 'living on tick' as never before in our history.

By rejecting the very idea of society you have widened all the divisions among our people – between North and South, between rich and poor, between the healthy and the sick. The family has suffered worst. Twice as many babies are now born out of wedlock. More than twice as many families are homeless, and many of those with homes are saddled with crippling mortgages. London and Liverpool are now dirtier than Milan and Naples. Violent crime has soared; only Turkey now has a higher proportion of its citizens in jail. The world now sees Britain as the home of the lager-lout and the football hooligan.

Your ideology, with its insistence on national sovereignty, has been disastrous for Britain's position in a world which is now feeling its way towards an international society. The globalisation of the financial markets, the multinational corporation, and the networking of industry across national frontiers have already set severe limits to the effective sovereignty of all states. You may remember how, though you prevented Nigel Lawson from joining the European Exchange Rate Mechanism, you had to let him raise interest rates within forty minutes of the Bundesbank doing so – in the middle of your party conference, although he had just spent two thousand million pounds of our reserves to avoid it.

By isolating Britain in the European Community, in the Commonwealth, and in NATO, you have robbed us of all influence in international affairs just as the end of the Cold War faces us with new opportunities, and new dangers. Those in Eastern Europe who support your type of nationalism now threaten the new democracies with Balkanisation. The inevitable disintegration of the Russian Empire, as the peripheral republics seek independence from Moscow, could extend such Balkanisation to the Pacific.

Meanwhile in the Third World nationalism risks producing new wars in the Middle East and on the Indian subcontinent. Medium and long range missiles are spreading rapidly, and at least half a dozen more developing countries are on the point of producing nuclear and chemical warheads for them. Unless the United Nations is swiftly enabled to bring such proliferation under control it may soon be too late to prevent catastrophe.

You claim to have recognised that the new dangers to the global environment ignore all national frontiers. Can you not see that this is equally true of the new dangers to global stability? Besides the political dangers I have described, the world economy is now in danger of collapse. The magic of the market-place has produced a financial system so heavily dependent on excessive debt that it is alarmingly vulnerable to shock. The freedom of world trade is threatened not only by the widening gap between North and South but also by the divisions between Europe, North America and Japan.

There is indeed no such thing as a world society, so far. But it is desperately necessary to create one. Two chances of creating a world society have already been missed – after the First and Second World Wars. The end of the Cold War has given mankind a third. If we miss that, I do not think there can be another.

They say you are now prepared to think again about the Poll Tax. Please think again about the ideology which spawned it.

Yours sincerely,

[signature]

DENIS HEALEY, MP.

The Rt Hon. Denis Healey is MP (Labour) for Leeds East. He is a former Defence Secretary (1964-70) and Chancellor of the Exchequer (1974-79); Deputy Leader of the Labour Party (1980-83) and opposition spokesman on Foreign and Commonwealth Affairs (1980-87). He published his memoirs, *The Time of My Life*, in 1989.

KENNETH BAKER

Conservative Central Office.

Dear Neil,

At the time of writing, the polls show that the Labour Party appears credible once more – a far cry from its standing over the past ten years. Following the collapse of the Labour Government in 1979, the fratricide which followed, the electorally suicidal manifesto of 1983, your own accession as Party Leader, and the glossy but ineffectual campaign of 1987, you have finally steered the Labour Party to a position it last held 16 years ago – that of an apparently electable opposition to a Conservative Government.

But here lies the rub, for what your achievement actually represents is the triumph of appearance over substance. Management of one's Party is not a sufficient qualification for management of a nation. To achieve that, you need credible policies which will convince electors and commentators of both your earnestness and fitness for office.

Your much trumpeted Policy Review owed its favourable reception by the media to your Party's interpretation of its contents rather than to the contents themselves. An examination of what you actually hold out does not lend itself to the conclusion that Labour has changed in substance as opposed to appearance.

My biggest criticism is that the Policy Review still fails to come to terms with the realities of the 1990s. You seem to think it sufficient to return your Party to the policies of the 1960s – ironically that same Wilsonian socialism against which you always rebelled.

Well those interventionist policies not only failed Britain, they were repudiated by most of the radical socialists who occupy seats on the backbenches behind you. A return to milk and water socialism won't satisfy them. They want the red-blooded version. While you wave the red rose they wave the Red Flag. And these are the people on whom you would have to count for any Labour majority in Parliament. What price "moderation" then?

However, while your Party has been in purdah, advised by its marketing experts on which policies are liked and which ones disliked, which policies are to be kept and which ones ditched, the world has changed dramatically around you. Just at the time your Party emerged with its new Socialist agenda, the people of Eastern Europe rose against their Soviet imposed masters and voted for a non-Socialist agenda. The temper of the times sweeping the continent of Europe is a temper which rejects precisely those nostrums and principles you now hanker after. Ironically, for all your efforts to develop policies which go with the grain of popular feeling, you have launched them at a time in history when the very philosophy of Socialism itself goes against the grain.

The key principles on which your Party stands – state control over the commanding heights of the economy, state intervention to direct economic and industrial resources, the dominance of the state in providing housing and education services, these are the very features of socialist economies against which the peoples of Poland, Hungary, Czechoslovakia, Romania and East Germany have rebelled. Just as you announced your intention to move Britain away from the market economy, so those other nations are seeking advice from Britain's Conservative Government about how to achieve such an economy. Even Mikhail Gorbachev, in the biggest ever reversal of Soviet domestic and economic policy, has pronounced the principles of a socialist economy as dead. He is now calling for market solutions. His country is atrophying under an inefficient centralised and bureaucratised economic system, a version of which you want to create anew in Britain.

The clearest indication of your unwillingness to abandon old dogmas came when you told *The Independent* that there was nothing for which you could give credit to the three Conservative Governments since 1979. Since those Governments removed trades union immunities, privatised major industries, put the brake on public and local government spending, introduced education and housing reforms, reduced Britain's international debt, and placed control of inflation at the centre of economic policy, it is a fair assumption that you want to lead Britain in the opposite direction. Well, why don't you come out and say so?

A huge question-mark hangs over other key policies too. As an unrepentant supporter of the Campaign for unilateral Nuclear Disarmament you now ask everyone to believe that you have become a multilateralist. You say you accept that Britain should continue to possess its existing nuclear weapons. You do not say whether you would replace them as they age and decay. You don't say whether you would be prepared to use them, which of course you have to say if Britain's nuclear deterrent is to remain credible. You do not explain why you have abandoned your emotional abhorrence of nuclear weapons in order to embrace them.

But then some of us don't believe you have actually changed. We think you remain as convinced an opponent of nuclear deterrence as you ever were. It is just that you realise you would never stand a chance of being elected into Government if you openly admitted what you truly believe.

That refusal to come clean has now been elevated into a strategy. Of late, your leadership of the Labour Party has been characterised by a most uncharacteristic silence. Reticence has replaced rhetoric. Even when you are allowed to talk a lot you actually say very little. I really think voters expect rather more from their would-be leaders.

As you know, I have written to you regularly putting various questions about Labour policies, questions which deserve serious answers. Yet answers there have been none. You seem to treat such questions as an intrusion into private meditation. You seem to believe that if only you maintain a hermit-like silence for long enough then the Labour Party will inherit the mantle of Government. But the only effect of your silence is to leave nobody knowing what you in your heart of hearts truly believe. People thought they knew some years ago. Now you seem to stand for nothing. Today, people are asking, 'Who *is* the real Neil Kinnock?' 'What does he *really* believe?' A hollow centre neither inspires the country nor addresses its problems.

The attributes required by anyone who aspires to become Prime Minister are clear political principles, the conviction to hold to those principles and to argue for them persuasively; the courage to stick to policies even when these may be unpopular; the ability to grasp the detail of policy, and the personal dignity which befits the holder of our nation's greatest elected office.

Within two years, the voters of Britain will make their own judgement as to whether you and Labour measure up to the expectations they have of would-be governing Parties. Even were I not the Chairman of the Conservative Party, I would still feel that too many unanswered questions remain about what you would do with the power you seek. It still remains for you and the Labour Party to answer all the tough questions – if you can.

Yours sincerely,

Kenneth

KENNETH BAKER, MP.

The Rt Hon. Kenneth Baker is MP for Mole Valley, and Chairman of the Conservative Party. He is a former Secretary of State for Education and Science.

WILLIAM RODGERS

Kentish Town,
London NW5.

Dear Neil,

You will be surprised to hear from me. We had only a nodding acquaintance during our thirteen years together in the House of Commons, and we haven't spoken since. But all credit to you for making the Labour Party look like an acceptable candidate for government once again and for building a good team around you. I am concerned by the suggestion that you would put *all* your elected Shadow Cabinet into office, and you cannot possibly make Gerald Kaufman your Foreign Secretary after his shameful performance over Hong Kong. But John Smith has the ability to make an impressive Chancellor of the Exchequer – a key role at any time – and a number of your bright, younger people could become effective Cabinet Ministers.

So why am I writing to you now? Not, I'm afraid, because of confidence that you will shortly make it to Number 10. On balance, I expect a narrow Tory victory. But, win or lose, Mrs Thatcher's era is moving to its close. The real question for the 1990s is whether we shall again see a government of the centre-left.

Some of my friends are so incensed by Mrs Thatcher that they will vote to get rid of her at any price, whatever the alternative. I understand their feelings, but that is not my position.

In retrospect, I think she will be seen as a necessary event, a catharsis, in the body politic. I grudgingly approve of most of her privatisation-of-industry measures, and I agree broadly with the way she has handled the trade unions. And although I am appalled by the devastation she is causing to education and the NHS, both needed some radical new thinking.

No, my real quarrel with Mrs Thatcher is that she has made a virtue of the selfish, aggressive and philistine instincts in us all. As a result, we are a meaner, more divided and less tolerant nation.

But Mrs Thatcher has little time left, and her successor will have no difficulty in steering the Tory Party back onto the middle ground, to sighs of relief from dissident supporters. I know you are uncomfortably aware of this, believing that you can more readily beat Mrs Thatcher than Michael Heseltine or Douglas Hurd (my choice) or whomever it may be. But it is not sufficient for you to pray for her survival. You must lift your sights.

The fact is that a large part of the electorate is footloose. When the SDP was launched in 1981, it provided leadership for many men and women who were fed up with the two, old parties. In the 1983 election, the Alliance won 25.4% of the vote, only a few per cent less than Labour. In 1987, when you led a dazzling Labour campaign, for every three people who voted Labour, at least two voted for the Alliance. The growth of the centre has rested on profound economic, social and demographic changes, and these are continuing. If David Owen had not opposed merger, the Liberal Democrats would be winning by-elections today and chalking up at least 30% in the opinion polls.

Even now, the likely success of the Liberal Democrats in 1991/92 is being underestimated. All over southern England the Alliance was in second place to the Tories in 1987, and Liberal Democrats remain a major factor in local government. I would not be surprised if they ended up with a result quite like last time, giving them over 20 MPs. Who knows, Paddy Ashdown and his colleagues may hold the balance in the House of Commons and determine who is to be the next Prime Minister.

But that is not my point. For over thirty years I was a member of the Labour Party, and it is nearly ten years since I helped to create the SDP. I believe that the Alliance might have formed the government of Britain, and the Liberal Democrats have a lot going for them still. But if Labour can once again capture the middle ground and provide a centre-left government of conscience-and-reform, good luck to it. What I am asking – and this is why I am writing to you – is whether you can now turn Labour into a genuine social democratic party, speaking for all the people and not on behalf of any class or interest.

As I've said, for those of my friends who take a short-term view, anything is better than Mrs Thatcher. I am looking farther ahead. I would rather see a change of government postponed than a Kinnock administration collapse in tears and ashes.

I assume that we broadly agree about education, the health service and housing. You would find more resources for them and restore their priority in Government spending. As a private citizen, I would happily pay more in taxes if called upon (although not, I should warn you, for the sort of waste and incompetence I've seen from the Labour Council here in the London Borough of

Camden). As for the central problem of the economy, it is difficult to get things right, and I have no secret remedy. But a Labour Chancellor should do at least as well as John Major, provided he does not get in hock to the unions. No more social contracts, please!

This brings me to the major areas of policy on which you must move if you are to win my goodwill and, more important, that of moderate opinion in the country.

First – and this will come as no surprise – you will be desperately vulnerable to trade union pressure once the unions are released from the straitjacket of the Thatcher years. I remember that you sat on your hands during the Winter of Discontent which brought Jim Callaghan down. You were more anxious then to be popular with the Transport and General Workers' Union than to support your government. You were also the first Labour leader to be chosen by an electoral college in which the unions have the dominant voice.

Only someone who has served in Labour governments can appreciate fully the permeating influence of the trade unions at such times. Even if union leaders start with good intentions, they are always pushed from behind. The public sector unions in particular will negotiate every drop of blood out of you. You and your colleagues have little experience of negotiating and little taste for it. Loyalty to the unions (and the loyalty they have shown you), sentiment, guilt – all these emotions will come into play.

Don't misunderstand me. I strongly support the unions in their workplace role, representing their members over wages and conditions of work. They should also be free to sponsor Members of Parliament if they wish. But they are not good at separating their own day-to-day objectives from the long-term national interest, of which you must be the custodian. In the Attlee government Ernest Bevin held the line from within the Cabinet. There is no such towering trade union figure to help you today.

Breaking the institutional links between the Labour Party and the trade unions is your next, great task, and it needs to be done now. It will mean getting rid of the electoral college and adopting a new, one-member, one-vote system to elect your successor. It will mean a wholly individual membership for the Labour Party and an end to affiliated status. The block vote will disappear from Conference and with it millions of pounds of steady money. It will be a brave, bold step, and you will be tempted to settle for cosmetic gestures and half-measures.

The second major issue is electoral reform. This is no longer a tiresome, minority fad that Roy Hattersley can huff and puff about. Support is gathering momentum. Your own people in Scotland are quite keen on it. Many voters see the present system as grossly unfair, and others would regard PR as a litmus test of how genuine you are in wishing to abandon the more confrontational aspect of politics. At the election, one of your themes will be national reconciliation – working together after the divisive Thatcher years. Here is a marvellous opportunity to adopt a radical proposal consistent with this. You will also, incidentally, score with the business community, which sees PR as a means towards greater continuity in industrial policy. My advice would be to concede PR for European elections as a start, and announce a timetable for introducing it into local government and then Parliamentary elections.

Apart from PR, what is needed is a whole platform of constitutional reforms of the kind set out by Charter 88, including a Bill of Rights. Your present hesitation about this stems from the essential conservatism of the Labour Party. Break with the past, and you will make many friends.

This is a letter, not a Manifesto, and it is getting too long. It is time for me to finish, and I've said nothing about defence or Europe, where your better record is too recent to be entirely reassuring, or about Militant Tendency and the other hard-left factions which are still active in your party. As for your speeches, I'm afraid that you have yet to learn fully how to confront great issues with depth and statesmanship and really sound like a Prime Minister-in-waiting.

But I write because you have done better than I ever expected. The re-alignment of the centre-left in Britain is a great task, and someone must achieve it. We cannot have Tory governments for ever.

Yours sincerely,

Bill Rodgers

WILLIAM RODGERS.

The Rt Hon. William Rodgers was born in Liverpool and educated there and at Magdalen College, Oxford. He was an MP for 21 years and a Labour Minister for eleven, latterly in the Cabinet. In 1981 he was one of the SDP's founding 'Gang of Four'. He is now a Liberal Democrat.

DAVID ICKE

The Green Party,
London SW12.

Dear Mrs Thatcher and Mr Kinnock,

I have often seen you fire venom at each other across the despatch box and I am constantly bewildered at the scene. You seem to be under the impression that somehow you come from opposing directions. You don't. In most things that matter, you are the same.

Just like Mr Ashdown, Dr Owen, Mr Bush, Mr Gorbachev etc, etc, you both support an economic system that is destroying the world, a system that has taken just 40 years, 40, to dismantle much of what has taken 4,600 million to evolve.

You are all obsessed with the illusion that economic and human progress can only be measured in the amount of "economic growth" we have every year when it is this very growth that is *causing* the human and environmental mayhem all over the planet.

You might see different ways of spending the "wealth", you might even see different ways of sharing it out (though increasingly less), but you see the same way of creating it...by more production and more consumption with every passing year.

The Earth is finite, but the system you worship can see only infinity and that's why traditional politics is at war with the planet, at war with our children and at war with the future.

Two figures for you to contemplate when you call for more "growth". A three per cent growth rate year after year means we have to *double* what we produce and consume in 25 years; a three per cent growth rate over 200 years means that 200 years from now we will have to be producing and consuming more in a day than we currently are in a year.

Is that possible? Of course not – the Earth would be a wasteland long before that. So why are all your economic policies based on the idea that it can happen?

It is a nonsense and a suicidal nonsense and it is about time we saw some sanity from you and some courage to admit you have charted the wrong course and that things must change radically.

Have you ever asked what this "growth" you call for actually measures?

"Growth", Gross National Product, measures the amount of money that changes hands for goods and services in any year. That's it.

It doesn't measure who spends it or what on; nor the human and environmental costs of making and spending that money; nor the loss of irreplaceable resources used. It measures nothing like that – just the money that changes hands.

So every time there is a road accident and the emergency services are called, it adds to economic growth; and when someone is ill and needs treatment, the dearer the treatment the more the growth; and when there is an environmental or transport disaster like Chernobyl or Lockerbie or Kings Cross.

The system you are obsessed with adds the cost of all these things to the GNP and "growth" – it sees them all as desirable and positive. A greater folly it is impossible to comprehend.

And for this, the economic equivalent of a Stone Age club, we are destroying the Earth and ourselves in the process.

If a Martian had spent the last 40 years observing all this he would go home and report no sign of intelligent life.

While the rich countries (20% of the world's population) consume 80 per cent of the resources every year in the mad pursuit of "growth", parents in poor countries have to see a child die of preventable disease every *two seconds*.

While we go on chasing more and more for the few at the expense of the majority (yes the Labour Party, too, Mr Kinnock) an area of tropical forest the size of the Isle of Wight is destroyed or degraded every 24 hours. A similar area turns to desert. 200 million tonnes of topsoil, the very basis of life, is eroded, lost forever. Up to 50 species on the latest estimates become extinct and 100,000 people, nearly half of them children die through hunger – every day.

Growth hasn't done much for them has it?

And look at what growth has done in the rich countries. Every year there are more suicides, more alcoholism, more drug-taking, more depression and violence in all its forms and manifestations.

My goodness this is some successful economic system eh?

The first thing any sane government or opposition would propose is immediate increases in the cost of using natural resources. The more you use, the more pollution you create, and the fewer resources you leave for the future.

We don't cost natural resources as if they were finite, we cost them as if they were a bottomless pit. We don't cost them on the basis of the damage their pollution causes – we just pass those consequences on to the future. But the future is now today.

This will mean a re-distribution of wealth so the poor can afford the higher energy prices. They can't be made to suffer even more for a crisis that is not of their making.

It is not those without money that have wasted energy on the scale that has pushed us towards the abyss, it is those with money. Therefore they must bear the cost of that.

The immediate effect will be that industry and business will suddenly become far more efficient in their use of natural resources and they will start getting far more from far less as resource taxation is increased every year.

The moment we pass the point where primary resources cost more than recycled resources we will at last see recycling on a mass scale because it will become the cheapest option.

We must have products made to last as long as possible, not with built-in obsolescence; made of recyclable materials; made so they can be reconditioned and repaired.

All these things, along with many more I will be delighted to discuss with you, will slow down dramatically the speed at which we turn irreplaceable resources at one end into pollution at the other.

This means a whole new look at economics and our measurements of "progress". It will take great courage to put forward this new economic vision which bases its ambitions on enough for all and not far too much for some and none for the rest.

I know this message will make you, Mrs Thatcher, turn purple with rage and incomprehension. I know it will make you, Mr Kinnock, turn white at the thought of what it might mean in the short-term opinion polls which appear to govern all opposition policy.

But I'm afraid the game is up. It can't go on or we won't go on.

Growth for growth's sake is not only destroying the Planet and causing untold misery, it is being used, and has always been used, to avoid what we really need: a fundamental redistribution of wealth.

While we could palm them off with the line that poverty will be cured if only we have "more growth" we could justify the chasms between rich and poor. Now, with growth no longer possible because of environmental limits, that old line won't wash any more.

We need more growth to eliminate poverty? What, when the money needed to give everyone in the world – everyone – enough to eat, decent education, shelter and health care for a *year* is spent on arms every *two weeks?*

What nonsense. We need more fairness, we need more justice, we need more vision, that's what we need.

Come on, take a deep breath, summon your courage, let's have you. *Now.*

Yours sincerely,

DAVID ICKE.

David Icke is a Green Party Council Speaker. A former professional footballer and sports journalist, he founded the Island Watch pressure group and is the Green Party's prospective candidate for the Isle of Wight. His guide to Green politics, *It Doesn't Have To Be Like This*, was published by Green Print in 1990.

BRYAN GOULD

*House of Commons,
London SW1.*

Dear Neil,

Many commentators have challenged Labour to come up with a "big idea" to rival Thatcherism. I have little sympathy for this view. For a start I refuse to elevate the combination of nineteenth-century liberalism, saloon bar prejudices and rampant authoritarianism that make up Thatcherism to the status of a "big idea". But more importantly, I believe the search for a "big idea" misunderstands the nature of politics in a modern pluralistic society, where a whole host of issues, attitudes and perceptions make up the bald facts of electoral arithmetic. Both Stalinism and Fascism were big ideas, but events in Europe today suggest that the big idea is on the way out. Citizens now prefer a politics that makes space for ordinary people and their aspirations, rather than forcing them to fall in behind the onwards march of the big idea.

That doesn't mean, however, that Labour should give up the battle of ideas, or that we have as a party limited ourselves to small ideas. Labour's Policy Review is full of usefully human-sized ideas – many of which now dominate the political agenda.

A particularly good example of an important idea linking up many of the policy items in our review is our belief that Britain is over-centralised. Indeed following the changes in Eastern Europe, it is true to say that Britain is now the most centralised country in Europe with the exception of Albania. And Mrs Thatcher wants to keep it that way.

She has been determined to remove discretion, autonomy and power from local government and transfer it to Whitehall. These prejudices mark her out as a politician of the eighties. The trend in the 1990s will be the exact opposite. There will be more decentralisation, not less, and we will increasingly learn the lessons offered to us by our European partners.

One decentralised dimension that exists across Western Europe is completely missing from Britain, and that is a regional tier of government. Its creation is now long overdue and is the key to dismantling the over-centralised British state, and making it closer to the people.

Although our plans for devolution to Scotland are now clear and are an early legislative commitment, we still have work to do in developing the detail of our plans for England and Wales and persuading the public that we mean business. However, we are making steady progress, and it is right that I report on our work to date.

First of all, we will make it clear that regional government will not be a tier of local government. The whole rationale is to push power downwards and outwards from Westminster and Whitehall, not remove it from the Town Hall. This is decentralisation, not regional centralisation. This also means that regional government is not a substitute for, or an alternative to, restoring respect and autonomy for local government.

Secondly, we do not want to impose a further tier of government, and we must therefore create a single tier of all-purpose district authorities below the regional tier. Of course in the metropolitan areas there is already a single tier, but in the shires, apart from one or two relatively minor, and mostly regulatory or strategic functions, currently exercised by the upper tier of local government that will best go to the regional level, one council will exercise virtually all the powers currently shared between two tiers at present.

Thirdly, I am not attracted by the notion that regional governments should have different powers in different parts of the country. This does not mean that regional councils will want to exercise their powers in the same way and for the same reasons. The priority in the North East may well be economic development, while in the South East, it may be containing over-heating, and congestion. But this should not mean that the Westminster Parliament legislates at times for the UK as a whole, at times for just for England and Wales, and at other times just for south of the River Trent.

Fourthly, we need to decide whether devolution and decentralisation come overnight or whether they take place in stages. I hope that we are in a position to make rapid progress on the creation of a regional tier, because I believe it is central to the economic renaissance of the country. Britain must be got back into balance. I am also a great enthusiast for devolving powers to deal with transport as I believe this is rapidly becoming the worst problem in my area of the country – London and the South East.

This brings me to those who say that there is no demand for

devolution in the South East. There is an obvious retort to that which I have heard from many Northern and Scottish politicians which goes: 'That's hardly surprising, since we already have government for the South East, from the South East, by the South East.' It's a good line and is partly true – although the growing congestion and deteriorating quality of life in the South East suggests otherwise. However, it is certainly true that you do not find the question of a parliament for the Home Counties spontaneously raised on the doorstep. This, however, should not be a problem for the Labour Party. It's a confusion between form and content.

The demand for a Scottish Parliament did not come about because the Scottish people wanted their own mace and the chance to create slightly ridiculous parliamentary customs of their own, but because decisions affecting the lives of Scots were not being taken by people accountable to, and elected by, the Scots. The argument must be the same in England. The question is not 'do you want a regional tier of government?', but 'do you want to have a say in how the health service is run locally? Do you want a more prosperous local economy? Do you want a public transport system that takes you where you want to go when you want to go?'

Labour has now eliminated the negative, now we must accentuate the positive. Decentralisation can be made an important part of our appeal. I am sure it has a major part to play in propelling you into Downing Street after the next election.

Yours ever,

BRYAN GOULD, MP.

Bryan Gould is MP (Labour) for Dagenham. He is currently Shadow Secretary of State for the Environment in Neil Kinnock's shadow cabinet and a member of Labour's National Executive. He is the author of *A Future for Socialism* (Jonathan Cape, 1989) and *Socialism and Freedom* (Macmillan, 1985).

DAVID BLUNKETT

Sheffield.

Dear Mrs Thatcher,

So you want to 'sweep socialism from the face of Britain'. The problem for you is your failure to recognise that socialism is not the carbuncles which have given it a bad name but a much more deep-seated commitment by so many people to the belief that they are social beings. In other words, they believe that we are inter-dependent in a complex and harsh world, where as individuals we are vulnerable but gain strength by acting together. Social cohesion springs from the understanding that in a civilised and caring world, we need to share our talents and work together to improve the world around us.

There is no doubt that you have considerable strengths. Your conviction and determination have won you many friends, but paradoxically they have also been your downfall. For whilst you struck a chord with many people in your verbal assault on bureaucracy and the power of the central state, you were driven by ideological motives which led you to centralise political power and go beyond the antagonism which people felt for old-fashioned collectivism.

In seeking to transform economic and social structures to place emphasis on "economic democracy" as opposed to "political democracy", you needed to use the latter in order to press home your own values and principles. This had the dual impact of disengaging from commonsense support for key parts of the productive economy, whilst intervening as never before in the public arena.

Unlike in other free market economies, you are opposed to substantial investment in education and training and in the manufacturing sector, but have been over zealous in your wish to intervene in dismantling public services. From the privatisation of the water industry through to the imposition of the Poll Tax, you took steps which disturbed and upset long-standing and instinctive values which you mistakenly believed had been undermined or even destroyed by the past decade of radical right-wing change.

The Poll Tax embodies two mistakes which have proved

fundamental in changing people's perceptions of their own self-interest in allying themselves with the Thatcherite revolution. The first is incompetence. The chaos and mismanagement which have surrounded the imposition of a new local government tax and the 11 years of muddle and interference in the local government arena which preceded it, have done little to endear the British people to your vision of a future based on individualism and unfettered economic self-reliance. Whilst the sale of public assets and tax cuts have given the substantial feeling, and for many, the reality, of greater personal well-being, the Poll Tax has inflicted pain on far more people than you ever intended. This, coupled with high interest rates, affected the very home owners who had believed you to be their champion.

Lack of manufacturing competitiveness and even capability have made a significant contribution to the poor performance of Britain in respect of currency rates. The property-led development boom is over for many people in the heartland of Conservatism and non-realisable assets have become more difficult to maintain. As a consequence, people have started to reappraise their own perspective on the economic and political competence of the Government.

The second fundamental mistake of the Poll Tax is that it strikes at the very heart of the values which British people hold dear and which you sought to destroy. You have evangelised the views of people like Friedrich Hayek who believe that 'obligations cannot exist to society as a whole but only to known and identifiable individuals'. Whilst no one would disagree that we have a responsibility for our family and friends, the idea that we do not also have some obligation or responsibility for others is unacceptable to those who believe in social cohesion.

At the height of the Industrial Revolution in Britain, people came together within their communities to meet need and to make provision which was not attainable through the operation of the free market. By introducing a Poll Tax which seeks to individualise payment into a flat rate charge, you struck a blow at the acceptance of mutuality and inter-dependence, and at the same time, attempted to depress spending on the very services which so many people continue to believe are essential.

You have ceased to identify with the basic aspirations of the British people. Even your own elected Conservative councillors have found it unacceptable to implement the cutbacks in key services such as education and social service provision which would have been necessary to reduce Poll Tax levels to the original figure of an average of £178 in 1986, which by 1989 had become £278, and by 1990 has become a real average of £363 per head.

In other words, the electorate *want* decent public services and whilst, quite rightly, they do not wish to return to over professionalism and unnecessary bureaucracy, they do not embrace your vision of an unfettered market economy, where individuals and families fend for themselves.

One final irony is worthy of mention. The tremendous changes which have taken place in Eastern Europe are not seen by the British people as the death of democratic socialism but as the welcome departure of authoritarian communism and the feared and threatening totalitarianism of centralist dictatorship. As that fear disappears, with it goes the ability to hold up the traditional threat of the "Red Menace". Far from socialism being swept from Britain, Europe and the World, there is now an opportunity to meet the challenge of the 21st century by linking enterprise and innovation with the attainment of social objectives and the protection of our environment and quality of life.

Some of the measures you have taken have brought great harm to millions of people and caused great damage to our productive industry. But you have undoubtedly made all of us face squarely the world as it is, rather than as we would wish it to be. We look to the future wiser and more determined than ever to win people over to a more caring, compassionate and optimistic world than the one you will leave behind.

Yours sincerely,

DAVID BLUNKETT, MP.

David Blunkett is MP (Labour) for Sheffield Brightside, a member of the NEC of the Labour Party, and the party's spokesman on Local Government and the Poll Tax. He was a member of Sheffield City Council for 18 years, and Leader of the Council for seven years. He is co-author (with Bernard Crick) of *Aims and Values* and (with Keith Jackson) of *Democracy in Crisis*.

ALAN PLATER

London NW3.

Dear Mrs Thatcher,

This, from memory, is the second time I have written to you.

The first time was soon after your election in 1979. I don't know how clearly you recall election pledges but one of yours was 'to eliminate wastage in public expenditure' – the words may not be exact, but the sense is clear and, I'm sure, matches the spirit of your intentions at the time.

The first tangible result of this policy was the withdrawal of the traffic warden (or lollipop man, to use the cheerful vernacular of the times) from the road outside the school then attended by two of my children. It was, and is, a very busy road, especially at commuter times, as eager motorists rush to work. Whether they are pursuing the market forces, or are pursued by them, is a fine point requiring analysis by greater philosophers than you or I.

You did not reply to the letter, nor was the traffic warden restored, and there have been accidents on the road.

I later wrote to Cecil Parkinson after he mouthed grotesque inaccuracies about CND during a television interview. To his credit, he *did* reply. He did not answer the points in my letter, and he totally misunderstood a modest joke in my penultimate paragraph but it is, as you must have observed, an imperfect world.

All that being so, there seems little point in engaging in policy discussions. Instead, let me tell you a story first told to me by a friend in Newcastle upon Tyne almost thirty years ago. I don't suppose you hear too many stories on your daily round.

The story.

After a shipwreck, a dozen people – men, women and children – are marooned in a lifeboat. They know the direction of the nearest land and they have limited supplies of food and water.

They have a decision to make – and this is where the fun really starts because you, the audience, have to decide how the story ends. What larks!

Do they:

1. Share the food, the water, and the work, and find their way to land by sensible cooperation?

Or:
2. Do they fight each other, kill each other and eat each other, so that in the end one strong man or woman, the sole survivor, reaches the dry land alone?

Most people choose Option 1, which is interesting since – give or take the odd semantic/ideological quibble – it is the socialist solution; whereas Option 2 – give or take similar quibbles – is the Monetarist/Market Forces/Capitalist approach, and finds few friends.

I shall be sending a copy of this letter to Mr Kinnock who, I know, is interested in such concepts.

Do not feel obliged to reply to *this* letter but regard it as a friendly contribution to the free flow of ideas – the good, the bad, the dangerous and the crazy – vital to the health and humour of a civilised democracy.

Yours etc.,

Alan Plater.

ALAN PLATER,
Voter.

Alan Plater is a novelist and writer for theatre, films and television. His work for theatre includes *Close the Coalhouse Door;* his TV work includes three *Beiderbecke* series, *The Fortunes of War* and *A Very British Coup*. Work in prospect includes *Sweet Sorrow* (for Hull Truck) and *Going Home* (for Live Theatre, Newcastle).

Lisa Appignanesi is a writer, television producer, and formerly Deputy Director of the Institute of Contemporary Arts in London. She is co-editor (with Sara Maitland) of *The Rushdie File* (1989) and author of *Simone de Beauvoir* and *Cabaret: The First Hundred Years* amongst other books. She edited the ICA's Documents series, including *Postmodernism* and *Novostroika*, and for television was executive producer on *England's Henry Moore* and *Seduction*.

LISA APPIGNANESI

London N19.

Dear Mr Kinnock,

Even these days one looks to a future Prime Minister (and you will have my vote) for some form of leadership, some form of guidance. Yet on an issue which has in this last year been not only of national, but also of global import, you have been oddly silent; indeed, though I hesitate to use moral terms, cowardly.

You have ducked the whole matter of the Rushdie Controversy.

It is clear that the Rushdie Affair, even before the pronounce-ment of Ayatollah Khomeini's deplorable *Fatwa*, split the Labour Party. Bernie Grant, Max Madden, Keith Vaz, Brian Sedgemore and later your own deputy, Roy Hattersley, ranked themselves, with one eye on electoral polls, on the side of the knee-jerk defenders of minorities and effectively wanted *The Satanic Verses* banned. Eric Heffer, Michael Foot, Clare Short and Mark Fisher spoke out on the side of freedom of expression and a liberal democratic society. But a split within the Labour Party is hardly a reason for its Leader's silence.

I am hardly for the silencing of disparate individual voices within a political party. But surely this matter called for a little guidance, a little clear thinking, a statement from the Leader of the Labour Party. Paddy Ashdown certainly didn't hesitate.

I would assume that the Leader of the Labour Party did not consider the Rushdie Affair merely a passing storm in a literary teacup. Ducking the issue won't make it go away. The controversy raises questions that go to the very heart of what liberal democratic society is all about. And hence to the core of what kind of society the Labour Party envisions for all of us, whatever our private faiths or lack of them. So, Mr Kinnock, please, a statement.

Is your multiculturalism of the kind which sings the romance of roots and blindly assumes that whoever speaks loudest on behalf of ethnicity and minorities must always and inevitably be on the side of the angels?

Or do you make distinctions between a genuine respect for different traditions and what in those traditions may be authori-tarian, absolutist, patriarchal; may stifle dissent – may in other

words be as inimical to various members of those minorities as it is
to any notion of a liberal social democracy?

Is your respect for "piety", for "faith" greater or lesser than your
respect for the long fought for values of the secular enlightenment?

I for one, and I do not think I am alone, would like to know.

Your colleagues in France, Messieurs Mitterrand and Rocard,
were quick to speak out in the wake of the *Fatwa* both against
clerical and religious obscurantism and against incitement to
violence and murder. They emphasised the secular character of the
French State, and affirmed the basic liberty of expression. Would
you, as Prime Minister, do the same for Britain? Or would you,
with an eye to the ballot box, sell out our writers – and with them
our Muslims, Christians, Jews and free-thinkers – and timidly
extend the blasphemy laws?

It may seem a little late to ask. But the issues the Rushdie
controversy has brought so blatantly and tragically into the open
won't go away. Where will Labour stand on questions of separatist
sectarian education? On women's rights within religious groupings?
Whom will Labour take to be the "representatives" of Muslims –
Islamist zealots backed by well-endowed foreign coffers or the less
easily heard but perhaps more representative individuals whose
cultural backgrounds are as diverse as those of Europeans?

And since Europe is on the agenda, where will you position
yourself on those who in certain quarters are beginning to be
known as the Islamic boat people, those who increasingly have to
flee repressive regimes and their inquisitorial procedures?

Will you dare to speak out in favour of human rights in Islamic
countries, especially when these are violated in the name of religion
and so-called national authenticity?

Please, Mr Kinnock, tell us. I think we'd like to know.

Yours sincerely,

[signature]

LISA APPIGNANESI.

PS. And am I to assume that a Labour Government would protect
Mr Rushdie in his enforced hiding as readily as a Conservative
Government has done? Despite some of your members' occasional
anti-intellectualism, occasional references to Mr Rushdie's supposed private wealth, I do trust that, if this is necessary, you will
indeed do so...

JOHN J. VINCENT

Urban Theology Unit, Sheffield.

Dear Mrs Thatcher,

In your lecture to the National Children's Home George Thomas Society in January, you said that the Victorians' initiatives into child care depended on three factors – first 'the commitment of one person inspiring many helpers'; second, 'the power of voluntary societies to pioneer new ventures'; and third, 'that the early reformers were almost all Christians, who saw such duties as an expression of their faith'.

You then spoke of the 'environment created by the values, standards and rules on which we base our lives', which you list as:

> First, that each person matters in God's sight and is therefore worthy of respect; second, the acceptance of those principles of right and wrong which are the foundation of the laws of this country, indeed of our whole way of life; third, meeting our responsibilities to care for those in our trust, especially those in need.

What we need is: 'a united and universal effort' to preserve and protect 'the environment of values':

> Such an environment is not bleak or forbidding. To observe the rules and courtesies of life is to show respect and consideration for all other people, each and every one. This environment starts in the family, for the very foundation of human happiness lies in the development of secure emotional relationships within the home.

Your basic argument is that the heart of Christianity is in the family, and values attached to the family.

There can be no question that the family is important. It is a feature of Christian life for many people. But it is not a distinctively Christian thing. Most major religions both emphasise the importance of the family, and also provide teaching concerning the sanctity of the family, the importance of parental presence and parental love, and the duties of children to their parents. Likewise there is strong opposition to the breaking of marriage vows, to adultery, and to divorce. And most religions also reluctantly provide ways of dealing with these regretted realities.

However, it is bizarre to argue that in a post-Christian or multi-faith age, the law of the land should seek to compel people against their will, to retain loyalty to family arrangements. And it is unfair to blame the churches, whose authority and significance the vast majority of citizens denigrate, for not instilling loyalty to the family in those outside the churches.

The problem can be put this way: The creation of a secure and loving family remains the ideal of most Christian parents, and is achieved by many people, both Christian believers and others. Equally, many other arrangements not normally described as "family" provide security and love.

Yet this is not the distinctive contribution of Christianity. Christianity has always insisted upon the care of the victims of any society. In our time, this applies to the bewilderingly growing mass of people in need: abused children, teenagers, unmarried parents, lone parents, unemployed, aged, disabled and those in poverty or educational deprivation. Many such people are themselves in a "cycle of deprivation", so that improvement of their lot in one area of deprivation in their lives will not in fact change their total condition, as the deprivation in so many other areas of their lives totally weighs them down.

So, Christianity holds to the sanctity of the family first for its own adherents and for the wider society. But it also sees itself called to continue the ministry of Jesus in including in the Family those who are outside the family system – the deprived, the deserted, the victims. All such people come to be the special responsibility of Christians and Christian organisations.

Furthermore, such care must not visit punishment on the victims of misfortune. The victims are already grossly disadvantaged because of the experiences they have gone through, and the situation in which they now find themselves. Therefore an overflowing concern and love is necessary, on the Christian view. Christian relief organisations like the National Children's Home are involved in this. But this is love, not law.

The Christian hope and impulse is towards securing a full life for all people. At times, the world being what it is, the family and those who support it have to be "used" in order to secure the wider full life for others. Much is expected from those to whom much is given. The Christian impulse is therefore not towards the protection of the nuclear family, but rather towards the extension of its benefits so that as far as possible all people are brought into human and humane family. That becomes a test-mark for politics from the Christian point of view.

How does all this relate to current policies?

1. Family arrangements cannot be equated with legally imposed obligations.

2. What you call 'caring for those in our trust, especially those in need', is a test of the truly Christian character of the family. The question must be how far government as well as voluntary societies make this possible.

3. Likewise, it is the task of voluntary organisations. So that a legitimate test of political policies would be: How far is this facilitated? Our experience in the voluntary sector is this. First, that voluntary giving in no way compensates for the amounts of money that public services have lost through tax cuts for the rich. Second, that voluntary organisations are being forced more and more to undertake the routine caring for those in need which it had been the consensus of civilised society to care for through state-supported institutions. This is even now changing the spirit and demoralising the workers in those organisations.

4. In the situation of increasing calls for care among the needy in our society, a wholly new approach is needed to secure a full life for all. This needs a massive input of finance and new services, based on a new philosophy of wholeness for all. So many policies at present are moving in the opposite direction. The "family" of humanity is broken by current divisive policies.

We need a fundamental change in basic political philosophy which goes *first* for the securing and protection of fullness of life for all our citizens. This is a Christian impulse, and belongs essentially to the well-being of the nation.

It is important here to bring the debate about enterprise into the picture.

Obviously, human enterprise is an essential part of being human. But there is an inherent oddity, not to say an intentional hypocrisy, here. On the one hand, 'There is no such thing as society, there are only individuals and families'; on the other hand, welfare corporately administered is suspect. We must therefore return people to the community to be cared for there. But how can a community which is only a collection of individuals and their families be expected to have any interest in caring for other individuals? A philosophy of privatised humanity and nuclear family has as its main aim the fortress mentality of self-help and restricted care, of "looking after one's own", which precisely – and intentionally – protects one from the ravaging expectations of others out there in the community or the society who might have designs on one's own resources, threaten one's family circle and even assume that just because they were human beings they might legitimately have a claim on our humanity.

The enterprise culture of the 80s is supposed to be leading into the caring culture of the 90s. But there are so far no indications that this is happening. And government policies continue unerringly to make the divisions in our society greater.

One is compelled to ask a very serious question. If, as my experience shows, the *effect* of so many current policies is to push the poor further into poverty, then one must ask: Is this result intentional? I have myself consistently given the Government the benefit of the doubt. In the fourth letter I wrote to you as Prime Minister on 15 December 1989, I said, 'I do not myself believe, and I have constantly said this, that the present government intends this greater disparity between rich and poor. Nor does it intend to cause poverty. Yet the tragic result of its policies has been to cause poverty.'

Yet legislation continues to be passed which renders the plight of the poor even worse. The starving of resources in poor areas for health, education, public services and general infrastructure result in increasingly bleak levels of deprivation, quite apart from the iniquitous Poll Tax.

In a word, enterprise does not lead to the common good. The "trickle down" theory does not trickle money down to the poor. The "echelon advance" theory does not move the poorest echelons one inch.

There is an additional problem. The Government claims to be the friend and encourager of enterprise. Everyone is expected to do their best to join the enterprise culture. Indeed, everyone is encouraged to do so by tax concessions. But not the poorest. It becomes, under present arrangements, increasingly impossible for the poor to cease to be poor. If you are poor you even get loans to buy essential things like cookers or bedding, so that you are not only poor but in debt – this is called the Social Fund.

The conclusion is inevitable. The rich need tax incentives to make them make money. The poor need tax victimisations in order to...In order to do what? In order to punish them?

Is there a deliberate and vicious plot on the part of your Government to render it all but impossible for those in the lowest strata of society ever to get out of them? Many politicians have been quoting assessments that between 10% and 20% of the nation belongs to a more or less permanent underclass. The label is as objectionable and insulting as the phenomenon.

But now we seem to take it for granted. Social benefits are allowed to all those "in the greatest need", to those who "slip through the system". But those benefits are at such a low level that one is compelled to believe one of two things. Either they are intended to be punitive, as ways of disciplining the poor and ensuring that people do anything they can to save themselves from falling into the abyss of poverty. Or they are intended to keep the poor poor. They are designed to compound poverty so that it becomes destitution. All that is then needed is the separation of areas of the destitute, under proper controls and effective policing.

Rising transport costs prevent the poor from emerging from the ghettoes. Neighbourhood Watch schemes protect society from them if they do, and schooling and social services and leisure provisions are cut down to a minimum or priced beyond their means.

Enterprise must now become the open door for all, and not the means of social separation. And enterprise must become enterprise for the common good. Things are worth doing not just if they bring profit, but if they bring greater quality of life for the greatest number.

Yours sincerely,

John J. Vincent.

REV. DR JOHN J. VINCENT.

Rev. Dr John J. Vincent is Director of the Urban Theology Unit in inner city Sheffield. As President of the Methodist Conference (1989-90), he held forums on his book, *Britain in the 90s*, and pursued this in correspondence with Mrs Thatcher. This letter is adapted from a lecture he gave in the House of Commons on 3 April 1990.

DANIEL EASTERMAN

Newcastle upon Tyne.

Dear Mr Kinnock,

Past decades have witnessed exciting developments in several areas previously relegated to the sidelines of public concern. There is now relatively open debate about nuclear energy, pollution, the food chain, and other environmental issues, and it seems clear that no party can any longer afford to ignore such matters.

Yet there is one crucial area that has doggedly resisted efforts to bring it into the mainstream of public debate. That area is health. You may think it perverse or facetious to say so: superficially, few topics have been as hotly debated in recent years. But not a single debate, in or out of the House of Commons, has even begun to address the real issues affecting public health. I believe a Labour government would put the interests of the public at large before those of business or powerful lobbies, and so I address these few words to you, in the hope that you may at last pioneer a fresh and radical debate.

For there has been no debate. In all the manifestos, in all the conference speeches, in all the acres of newsprint about salmonella and listeria, acid rain and nuclear fallout, lead in the atmosphere and condoms on the beaches, not one word, not one syllable about the billions of pills, the oceans of serums, the gallons of vaccines, the tons of tranquillisers, antibiotics, anti-inflammatories, anti-depressants, steroids, and sundry immuno-suppressant gunge with which the medical profession pumps, injects and smears us. Not a word. Total, inexplicable silence.

What controversy there has been has touched exclusively on the mechanics of the health system: 'Save the NHS', 'privatise the NHS', 'rescue our local hospital', 'opt out', 'opt in', 'rationalise the system', 'pay the nurses more'. The sabres rattle on, but nobody stops for a moment to ask: 'Would even a radical overhaul of the system make the slightest difference? Would lives, in the aggregate, be saved? Would we be a healthier people? Would the public stop smoking, driving fast, eating hamburgers and chips?' Not once has anyone dared challenge the received wisdom that modern medicine is good for us and that more medicine means better health.

The simple fact is that neither the introduction of a National Health Service in Britain nor the perpetuation of privatised medicine in other countries has done much to improve the health of populations. Radical critics of medicine like Ivan Illich have even argued that the medical establishment presents 'a major threat to health', that more medicine may be synonymous with more illness.

In spite of vastly increased expenditure on hospitals, drugs, and high-tech medicine, we still have some of the worst death rates in the world from lung and breast cancer and heart disease, one of the lowest life expectancies in the developed world, and a rate of chronic illness that affects about one-third of the population. Chronic and degenerative conditions have reached epidemic proportions, yet study after study has shown that pouring more money into conventional medical services has at best a marginal effect and benefits no one but doctors and the pharmaceutical companies.

But the voices that dare to criticise the value of modern health care have gone almost unheard in the corridors of power. Why should that be? We have learned to criticise received wisdom in almost every other area. But to challenge the effectiveness of scientific medicine seems to be the last unbreakable taboo.

The media persist in portraying modern medicine uncritically. Doctors, unlike lawyers, architects, politicians, academics, or the members of any other profession, are curiously and perversely immune to outside criticism. Open debate and public account-ability in medicine are virtually unthinkable. But if the critics are right, no amount of tinkering with distribution or organisation will make things better. If medicine is really part of the problem, more of it will only serve to make us all sicker.

Is it not time for politicians to grasp this most painful of nettles? If health is to be improved in Britain, we must move rapidly from a medical model of health based on relieving symptoms to one that promotes positive health through changes in lifestyle, diet, housing, and working conditions. These are the very changes that defeated infectious illness in the last century. A truly caring government would address itself to them today as one of its greatest priorities. New legislation is desperately needed to tackle the problems of food processing, additives, irradiation, smoking, and the links between poverty and ill-health. Preventive medicine would save both lives and money.

In medicine itself, radical changes are needed to reduce the growing rates of iatrogenic (doctor-induced) illness, weighing the benefits of expensive operations and costly machinery against simple preventive measures, restricting the use of synthetic drugs, re-examining the value of procedures like mass vaccination, and encouraging a much greater role within the health service for alternative therapies.

The possibilities inherent in mainstream alternative medicine alone are enormous. To take a simple example: the Marylebone Health Centre, the only NHS clinic to combine orthodox with complementary treatments, has recently published figures to show a drugs bill reduced by about 65%. Applied throughout the health service, dramatic savings could be made, while patients would benefit at every level. And yet both sides of the House acquiesce in the irrational opposition of the medical/pharmaceutical lobby, eager to preserve their monopoly over health care.

Current policies favour the medical establishment, threaten the removal of many natural remedies, and, after 1992, may lead to draconian restrictions on practice by even well-qualified alternative therapists. I believe that this flies in the face of common sense. If you care about public health – and I am convinced you do – please use your influence to initiate a deep and lasting change. I am certain that the government which shows it possesses the courage to make health, not sickness, the basis for its policies will go down in history as a government that really did achieve something lasting for every one of us.

Yours sincerely,

Daniel Easterman

DANIEL EASTERMAN.

Daniel Easterman is a writer and academic, and formerly lecturer in Arabic and Islamic Studies at Newcastle University. His novels include *The Seventh Sanctuary*, *The Ninth Buddha* and *Brotherhood of the Tomb*. He is a prominent advocate of alternative medicine, a council member of the Natural Medicines Society, Vice-Chairman of Friends of Homeopathy, and co-author of *The Health Crisis* (NMS, 1987).

SHEILA KITZINGER

*Standlake,
Oxfordshire.*

Dear Prime Minister,

There is tremendous emphasis in the media today on the glamour of high-tech medicine and the thrilling advances made in IVF. Childbirth is considered a domestic, female concern, along with cookery and potty-training. Yet a traumatic birth, one in which the woman is disempowered, is a political issue for many women for whom birth has been a kind of obstetric rape. Birth is a political issue not only because there are aspects that can be statistically enumerated, but because the quality of the birth experience is important for women, their partners and their babies.

Regionalisation of care so that women have little choice but to give birth in large high-tech hospitals, the closing down of small GP units, the running down of the home-birth service – the obstetric take-over of birth – has meant that women travel long distances for care, and often have no personal relationship with caregivers. A woman in labour may encounter 30 or more different staff members flitting in and out of her room. Birth is treated as if it were a road accident or an appendectomy. If she is lucky there is someone there to hold her hand while professionals get on with the job of delivering a baby.

Hanging flowery curtains and putting pictures on the walls – the patchwork quilt syndrome fashionable in many hospitals today – does not humanise childbirth. Only people do that. What matters is who controls the territory in which birth takes place. For those in control also control everything that happens in it. And it certainly isn't the women for whom the institution is claimed to exist.

The party I vote for will start listening to women, not exclusively to obstetricians and managers. We are tired of the top-heavy power structure of the health service, the sweet-talk, the blandishments, and the ways in which obstetricians assume responsibility for our bodies and our babies as if women were incapable of accepting responsibility.

Midwives and mothers are forming a new alliance today. We are concerned about the quality of care, the trigger-happy practices of cowboy politicians in their element only when using continuous electronic fetal monitoring, the oxytocin intravenous drip, and every other intervention they can think of to control women's wayward uteruses.

And in terms of policy in the NHS? We should cherish our small GP units and turn them into midwife-run birth centres even better than those now mushrooming all over North America in response to women's strong demands. The challenge is to provide this kind of care not only for women who are socially privileged and able to speak out and demand it, but for every mother. Women designated as "high risk" because they are at social and economic disadvantage especially need one-to-one midwife care in pregnancy, during birth and post-partum.

We should remove all the obstacles to home-birth that are put in women's way so that, instead of having to give birth in the public arena of a hospital delivery room, women have the opportunity of giving birth in the peace and security of their own homes.

We need to build up small midwife teams offering care both in hospital and at home, strengthen the community midwifery service and, as in the Netherlands, where 37% of births take place at home and at the same time childbirth is as safe as it can be, enable women to have genuine choice.

This amounts to a revolution in childbirth care. I believe that bold political action of this kind is the only way in which women can reclaim the experience of birth.

Yours sincerely,

Sheila Kitzinger

SHEILA KITZINGER.

Sheila Kitzinger is an author, social anthropologist and birth educator, and works with the National Childbirth Trust. Her books include *The Experience of Childbirth*, *The Experience of Breast-feeding*, *Pregnancy and Childbirth* and *Woman's Experience of Sex*, all published by Penguin. Her latest books are *The Crying Baby* (Penguin) and (co-authored with her daughter Celia Kitzinger) *Talking with Children About Things That Matter* (Pandora).

LUCY ELLMANN

London E2.

Dear Neil and Margaret,

Pardon the use of your prenomens but the subject I wish to discuss demands a certain degree of intimacy: it's tampons. Nicaragua, football hooliganism and the Poll Tax no doubt have their place, but so do tampons. And this place is of vital importance to the happiness of the nation. Or at any rate it's a busy cul-de-sac in the nation's pursuit of happiness.

It would be difficult to think of an area of more personal concern to the majority of your constituents than the vagina. I could wax lyrical on the advantages of having one, well fairly lyrical I'm sure, but this seems more the moment to voice a complaint or two. I'll try two.

Of the many ingenious properties of this organ, menstruation is the least valued or understood. Average citizens can't even pronounce the word, should they wish to, which they *don't*. The prejudice and mystery surrounding menstruation cannot be condoned, but, as it exists, I venture to bring up the little matter of what to do if this happens to be a bodily function one can call one's own. Leakages are socially unacceptable, and the best method of avoiding them – the tampon – is expensive. It costs money to menstruate. We pay VAT to menstruate! The cotton wool companies clearly see menstruating as an elite activity worthy of exploitation.

An MP recently took it upon himself to advise women interested in making an economy in this region to consider wearing nappies as, he believes, was the custom in days of yore. Take 1 Outsize Nappy. Arrange in Kite Shape. Place Woman's Bottom on Changing Mat. Pull Corner A through Legs. Then take Corners B & C and try to join above Belly. Affix Safety-Pin. Dress Woman in loose-fitting Garments in order to conceal Presence of Nappy.

Bloody rags lack a certain *joie de vivre*, to my *fin de siècle* mind. But perhaps this explains why there are so few women to be seen in the corridors of power: they're all in the Ladies' Room adjusting their diapers.

FREE TAMPONS NOW. Free tampons would act as an

incentive to women to curb their fertility in the over-populated days
to come. Free tampons would mean an end to all those hazy
garbled ads on television that so appal certain men. In fact, get rid
of certain men while you're at it.

Women could meet up for menstrual dream analysis sessions at
the tampon distribution centres, and be given a handful each of
assorted Maximum, Modicum and Minimum Flow, unbleached,
toxin-free, vaginal-environment-friendly tampons, after an hour
devoted to self-worship of a cheering kind.

I know it is probably politically ruinous to be seen to be
advocating menstruation in any way, but I urge you both to consider
those balmy days of your retirement, when you will mull over your
accomplishments. Would it not be comforting in your dotage to be
able to declare: 'In many ways I further enslaved the British people,
but at least I let tampons go free.'

Your devoted servant,

LUCY ELLMANN.

Lucy Ellmann is a novelist, short story writer and journalist. Her first novel *Sweet Desserts* (Virago/Penguin) won the Guardian Fiction Prize in 1988.

JO RICHARDSON

House of Commons,
London SW1.

Dear Margaret Thatcher,

When you became Britain's first woman Prime Minister in 1979 you had a golden opportunity to carry forward demands from women for greater equality. It is true that you had already said that the battle for women's rights had been largely won, but perhaps you were thinking of your own experience.

You had after all had a good state education. You had a supportive family; you went to university and became qualified in two widely differing fields – as an industrial chemist and as a lawyer. You had two children, but your family circumstances enabled you to employ a nanny. And because you had support and help you were able to develop a third career – politics. You were therefore able to exercise a choice about your own life. Good for you!

But almost as soon as you entered No. 10 you began to close the door to real choice for the rest of women by the policies you inflicted on the nation.

You cut local authority spending. Perhaps you don't know it but local authority provision is crucial to women with families. They depend on it for help in so many ways. In the provision of a decent education for their children and, for example, particularly for women who aren't well off, on free school milk and free school meals (oh dear, I'd forgotten that you had already, when you were a Minister at the DES, abolished free school milk). They depend on support in caring for elderly or disabled dependants – respite care, day care centres, homes for the elderly – cuts in which have forced many working women back into the home.

Did you know that one in eight women today are full-time unpaid carers, saving in the region of £2 billions of public money? They are then isolated and largely ignored, because local authorities can't afford the back-up and help which would enable them to exercise their right to work outside the home and to achieve some financial independence. You extended the Invalid Care Allowance, paltry as it is, from single women and married men to married women very grudgingly and only because the Government was forced to do so by the European Court.

Under-resourcing the National Health Service too has restricted women's choices. Long waiting lists for admission throw the responsibility on the woman in the home who must rearrange her life to care for a loved one who is ill or in pain. It is not only the patient who suffers on a three-year waiting list. The agony for the carer is also hard to bear.

Then you abolished the protective legislation which had been in place for decades to stop the exploitation of women at work. Far from seeking to tackle the discrimination against women at work with positive initiatives to end low pay, you cut back on Wages Councils, removed restrictions on hours, turned your back on part-time women workers battling for conditions more in line with full-time workers, and ended the 80s with the majority of women still earning less than three-quarters of men's average pay. What a wasted opportunity.

You have cut maternity provision, and refused to introduce the concept of parental leave which other countries have found useful in involving fathers in the upbringing of their children. You have frozen Child Benefit which is of such crucial importance to mothers, and often the only money which is allowed them. You have done nothing to initiate and promote good quality childcare except to exhort employers to provide workplace nurseries in the light of the forthcoming demographic changes requiring women to return to work.

You set up a Ministerial Committee on Women's Issues chaired by a man and with twelve Ministers of whom only three are women. That Committee has done nothing to work out a range of childcare options – local authority provision for the secure funding for pre-school play groups, under-fives, out of school schemes and good quality child minding. It took you five years to remove the tax on workplace nurseries – your favoured option – and then only in response to the wide campaign which had been waged against the tax. The only other issues which the Ministerial Committee seems to have looked at are domestic violence and rape in marriage, and in both cases the Committee hasn't yet come up with positive initiatives or sought to change the law to protect women.

You claimed that the budget of 1990 was a budget for women. The vast majority of women have gained nothing and some have actually lost. You haven't helped women houseowners who are saddled with high mortgage interest payments. You've made no concessions to women who have to pay the Poll Tax, and you've ignored the low paid, two-thirds of whom are women.

You've introduced the married couples' allowance – but what is the result? It doesn't affect very low paid women anyway, and where you have two earner couples the woman ends up paying more tax than the man. That's a funny kind of equality.

Why haven't you appointed any women from your own party into the Cabinet? You are still the only one. Why haven't you brought more women on to the boards and quangos which are still overwhelmingly dominated by men?

Why haven't you recognised that the majority of women start from a very low base, and need help and support to bring them to a standard where they can begin to take advantage of equal rights?

What you're doing is to ignore and marginalise the vast majority of women in Britain, whose talents, experience and wisdom could be of such value to themselves, to their families and to the community as a whole. What a waste of human resources. The recognition of women's talents could bring a really new flavour to life. Women's caring natures, so valuable to the family, could bring a new perspective to everyone's lives. Few women want to compete on male terms – which seems to be your philosophy. How many times have I shuddered to hear you referred to as 'the best man in the Tory Party'.

We are not like men: we have something different to offer.

You could have changed women's lives. But you've changed them for the worse. Any gains which women have made during the 80s have come about entirely as a result of their own determination.

Yours sincerely,

Jo Richardson

JO RICHARDSON, MP
Shadow Minister for Women.

Jo Richardson is MP (Labour) for Barking, Shadow Minister for Women, Chair of the Labour Party, and a member of the National Executive Committee. During her 15 years in Parliament she has fought many campaigns on women's issues, including childcare, training and retraining for women, and action against rape and sexual harassment, and has consistently led the fight against restrictions to the 1967 Abortion Act, defending both the Act itself and the rights of women to have access to fertility services. She is an active trade unionist, and Vice-President of CND.

MICHÈLE ROBERTS

London N19.

Dear Mr Kinnock,

This is a difficult letter to write. We don't know each other. You haven't asked me to write to you. You may never read this. I've never written a letter to a politician in my life, only long gossipy ones to friends. Yet I can't address you as I would my bank manager or the other powerful men I occasionally exchange correspondence with. If I believe that you represent the Party that listens, as you claim, then I'll tell you that although I have voted Labour all my life, I haven't always felt that Labour has listened to women. Least of all to women who are mothers.

Since the letter form has played an important part in the development of the novel in the West, I'll solve my difficulty of writing to you by turning my letter into a sort of fiction.

So. Here we are. You and Glenys and I have skived off work this warm sunny afternoon. We're sitting together on Hampstead Heath having a picnic. Sharing food and drink puts us in a friendly situation, makes it easier to talk. That's what I'm used to in my women's group: political discussions mixed up with the pleasure of eating. I've brought an omelette sprinkled with rosemary and onions and black olives, with plenty of olive oil, sandwiched between two halves of a loaf of delicious Italian bread, and some big fat tomatoes, and a large bunch of grapes. A bottle of cold white wine, some orange juice, and a cloth to lay it all on. We're sprawling in the long fragrant grass of an uncut meadow underneath a flowering chestnut tree. *Bon appétit!*

So let's contemplate pleasure, and how much pleasure for people continues to play a part in radical politics, Labour politics. In the much-maligned 60s and early 70s, we feminist women talked about wanting joy and pleasure in our lives and weren't ashamed of doing so, just as we also let ourselves examine the sources of the un-pleasure we so often encountered. One area that many women felt ambivalent about, and still do, was that of being mothers. The joy and satisfaction of having children is mixed up with the enormous stresses of trying to look after them well under the conditions imposed by a male-dominated and capitalist culture. The isolation, the struggle to make ends meet working in badly paid jobs, the lack of attention to mothers' and children's needs in the public sphere from housing to transport, the sentimentality disguising the lack of status and decent facilities for mothers, the guilt, the never being able to get it all right. Not much has changed. Women with male partners still experience themselves as single mothers. The men are out at work. Women are out at work too, then working frantically at home.

I wish the Labour Party would start to call for changes in the way we perceive paid work and childcare. Rather than supporting any calls for a return to full employment, which means full-time employment for men, with a lot of overtime necessary for making a decent wage, rather than encouraging the mothers of young children back to work with the carrot of more work-place nurseries or more flexible hours, I wish the Labour Party would encourage *men* to work *less*, so that they could become proper fathers. Certainly, let's have the community nurseries that we need and that we run, but let's also have shift work for all, part-time work for all, flexible hours for all, job-sharing for all. Let's release ourselves into the pleasure of spending and sharing time with our children in ways that suit their and our needs. As Michelene Wandor once put it in a poem: 'make all people/lovers and parents. Make/one word mean that.'

That's part of the revolution I want.

Have another tomato, Mr Kinnock. Have another fistful of grapes. Imagine this park, on a weekday afternoon, full of fathers caring for their children.

I'm dreaming aren't I?

Yours sincerely,

Michèle Roberts

MICHÈLE ROBERTS.

Michèle Roberts is a novelist and poet. She was born in 1949, and is half-French. Her most recent novel is *In the Red Kitchen* (Methuen, 1990) and her most recent poetry collection is *The Mirror of the Mother* (Methuen, 1986). She has also published essays, short stories, and a play.

SUE SLIPMAN

National Council
for One Parent Families,
London NW5.

Dear Mrs Thatcher,

The next ten years will offer all of us concerned with lone parents and their children a major opportunity to address the problems they face. Demographic changes mean that there is now room in the labour market for lone parents. The Government can decide to take measures which will enable them to enter and remain in work. It is unusual for a social problem to peak at the same time that the economy offers scope for addressing and overcoming it. Lone parents' poverty is such a problem.

It has not been all bad for lone parents under your Government. Your Ministers have done some useful things, but within your overall design of moving from your idea of "welfare dependency" to independence, lone parents as a group have suffered in the transition. To be fair to you, you have never described lone parents as "welfare spongers", but you have suggested that they have behaved in a way that has caused their own problems, and some of your closest adherents have concluded that they and their children should therefore pay the price for the wages of such sin.

We applauded your initiative to make defaulting fathers pay their child support, and were pleased to stand with you on the high moral ground that all parents have the responsibility to maintain their children.

We welcomed the Childcare Allowance that helps some lone parents qualify for work by undertaking Employment Training.

We supported the legislation that gave children born outside marriage equal legal rights for the first time.

In general we moved down the same path in wanting to get lone mothers off welfare support and into the world of work.

But we parted company on some significant issues: The core of the matter is who has responsibility for children? Is it the parents alone, or does the state enter into the equation? I know your preferred option would be to have parents take care of their children without recourse to state support. You have not been a friend to the notion of a universal child benefit as a recognition of the state's role in supporting family life. But it is hard to tell how far, and to what, your objections extend. Your Ministers have used the argument of "targeting" benefits to those who need help most to undermine the argument for general state support. The adherents of universal benefits argue that you wish ultimately to withdraw all state support: some of your more fanatical friends have publicly stated that any state support for the family weakens the moral fibre of the family. You have never gone so far.

There has, however, been much talk of "perverse incentives" within your administration. By which you mean that any positive measures to help groups with a particular problem has the perverse effect of adding to the numbers of that group by making membership of it more attractive. There may be issues where this fear is justified, but we have never believed, for example, that hoards of women flock to leave their husbands and partners in order to receive the extra £5.60 per week which the state gives lone parents in welfare support.

A major political question for your administration is a new social consensus on the balance between parental and state responsibility for children. Your approach on this will determine how well or badly lone parents ultimately fare if and when your vision of self-sufficient citizenship is realised.

So far, your Ministers refuse to grasp publicly the simple idea that to get lone parents off benefit and into work requires a co-ordinated, planned strategy with ongoing childcare support at its heart. They have talked sympathetically about women returners' childcare needs being supplied by employers and hope that this will cover lone parents. Whilst a number of higher flyers will be helped by employers, the majority of lone mothers are unlikely to receive such help as employers are costing the provision of childcare places against the replacement costs for highly trained professional staff – and not for those who will be on a low wage.

Your plans to get fathers to pay child maintenance will help many lone mothers to work – but when ex-partners are either un-employed or themselves on a low wage, there is simply not enough money to meet the costs.

Whatever your approach, getting lone mothers off benefit requires the state to make a contribution to their childcare. We have nothing against – nay, are positively in favour – of fathers doing their bit to the extent of their ability, but we know that for the less affluent a financial gap will be left that someone has to fill. We would argue that your hopes for increased economic activity, combined with your social policy should make you square up to the question.

In this, as in so many areas of your Government's policy, the major question is how far your Government is prepared to intervene in the workings of the market to ensure a better social outcome. Your battle cry is always *never*, but your back to the wall position is *as little as we can and never without maximum resistance.*

It is wearying for those of us lobbyists attempting to work with your Government's objectives to go on presenting a logical and coherent agenda upon which to have the debate. No doubt you would argue that it is good and sharpening intellectual practice for us to do so. It is not as if we are arguing for you to intervene in market forces in ways that totally conflict with your stated goals and objectives; but we cannot hide the fact that we are asking you to intervene. I would describe our request to you as intervening within market forces in the minimum possible way to produce the maximum possible good – for lone parents and their children, and for the Government's economic and social goals. It you are unable or unwilling to do so you will miss the opportunity that the next ten years give us to solve the growing problems of a major social group.

Our hope is that your moral intransigence will give way to a more considered and actively sympathetic response to achieving goals that you state to be your own. We suspect that this requires an examination of your own contradictions. This may be too much to expect of any politician.

Yours sincerely,

Sue Slipman

SUE SLIPMAN,
Director,
National Council for One Parent Families.

Sue Slipman is Director of the National Council for One Parent Families, and has successfully lobbied on areas of social and family policy, including the Family Law Reform Act 1987 and the Children's Act 1989. She was National Secretary and President of the National Union of Students from 1974 to 1978, and Negotiating Officer for NUPE (National Union of Public Employees) from 1979 to 1985.

BRENDA DEAN

SOGAT House,
Hadleigh, Essex.

Dear Neil Kinnock and Margaret Thatcher,

I am addressing this open letter to you both, jointly, as parents and politicians in the knowledge that the subject I am asking you to consider crosses party political boundaries.

Indeed, it is on an issue which determines the very future of our society. In my view, the mark of any society which claims to be civilised is the way in which it treats its young.

I would ask you both to set aside parliamentary time to introduce a Charter for Children. That is, not a simple Bill which deals only with one specific issue, but a comprehensive Bill of Rights for Children and Young People. It would need to embrace many areas and these I think, can best be illustrated by running through chronologically, from cradle to adulthood.

Infant mortality is highest amongst the poor and underprivileged with its spread varying also geographically. We must ensure that ante- and post-natal care is no longer determined by cash limits so that infant deaths are minimalised across all social classes in all parts of the country. Of course, that means improving education programmes for parents too, so that they make use of all that is available. It needs more health visitors to be recruited so that families get all the help they may need.

We need healthy minds too, as well as healthy bodies, so stimulating, pre-school nursery education is essential. Britain is among the poorest providers of state nursery places anywhere in Europe and that hampers development throughout childhood.

Sadly, toddlers and younger children are too often the victims of abuse by adults. At times, the justifiable public anger which follows child murders and brutal assaults is misdirected, away from the assailant to the agencies set up to prevent such tragedies. Undoubtedly mistakes are made, but under-resourced social service departments and agencies are intolerably stretched, making errors of judgement more likely. We must prioritise these services to reflect the world in which they are now operating and introduce legislation which gives child care agents the power to act as we say they should, when we enjoy the luxury of hindsight.

Child sexual abuse is now, at last, acknowledged to be a major problem which does exist – not only in the minds of a handful of doctors and social workers. For too long it was there but unreported or couched in euphemisms because the media believed we could not cope with the unpleasant facts along with our breakfast cornflakes. We need to fund massive research to identify and treat the root cause of these problems and again ensure that we have the resources to employ specialists to deal with them.

All these children are victims, at the sharp end of problems which adults transfer to them. But there are many children from good, loving, caring families who suffer different problems.

Our education system fails many of our children – those with learning difficulties that are not detected soon enough; those who have special needs which are not always catered for. We must remind ourselves again and again that the standard of education we provide determines the future for industry and our national wealth. But most importantly, it is a major determining factor in the quality of life for future generations.

Schools and colleges cannot be run as businesses. Success can not be measured by profitability in the form of a "gold star" for an arbitrarily set academic qualification. Success in education is about every pupil achieving their own potential – not aiming at someone else's level.

For this we must have properly staffed schools with teachers who are well trained for the task and well rewarded too. We must end the low status currently afforded the teaching profession and raise morale so that we keep the good, experienced teachers we have and attract some of our brightest people to the profession.

We have the dreadful contradiction at the moment where there is an attempt to impose standards nationally via the national curriculum while at the same time schools are being told that they must manage their resources locally.

Teenage agony, itself, is nothing new. But what is different today is the pressure under which young people find themselves as they prepare to enter the world of adulthood. They are courted by a consumer-obsessed society where the £20 note is King. For the most fortunate, cushioned by parental affluence, there is the shock of discovering that cash has to be earned. For the less fortunate, there is the constant struggle to achieve what advertisers tell them they should aspire to. No wonder so many give up.

Perhaps saddest of all are the children – for that is all many of them are – who run away from home, from school and from pressures they can no longer bear. They run not to something better in our perception, but to "cardboard cities" scattered throughout Britain, where too many degenerate into a life of drug abuse and perversion at the mercy of sordid adults.

Of course, childhood and adolescence is not like this for the vast majority. But you, as politicians, have a vital role as guardians. For you are guardians of the society in which these youngsters may flourish – or wilt, and even die.

You can set minimum standards which help determine the future for our young. Surely, there can be no greater cause for setting aside time and casting aside your differences. I urge you to do this.

Yours sincerely,

Brenda Dean

BRENDA DEAN.

Brenda Dean is General Secretary of the print union SOGAT '82. She is a member of the General Council of the TUC, Chairman of its Printing Industries Committee, and serves on several other TUC committees. When Rupert Murdoch moved his newspapers to Wapping, she led the union campaign to have the sacked Fleet Street print workers reinstated. Since 1988 she has served on the Council and Africa Review Committee of the Save the Children Fund.

MARINA WARNER

London NW5.

Dear Mr Kinnock,

The Natural History Museum has announced that it may have to start charging entrance fees to schools. This seems to me another kind of Poll Tax, levied on under-18s, another way of punishing people who have children and rewarding those who don't, another way of reproaching children for having wants and needs and no earning power to pay for them.

I would like you to reverse this punitive trend, when you and your party come to power. Some of the measures needed are incorporated in the EC's Social Charter, and I hope you will give them your full support, however much they cost. They include statutory rights for part-time workers, so that women, who often fit in mothering with necessary earning, are granted sickness benefits and pension possibilities on the same lines as full-time workers. Parental leave for both parents will help women who are considered unreliable employees because it is almost always the mother who stays home when the child is sick; if the father has a right to do so as well, the burden can be shared.

Child care services in Britain are the worst in Europe: even a country like Italy, with its Catholic tradition, has a widespread public programme of crêches and centres where working mothers can leave their children for as much of the day as they need. The Italians do not see this as neglect, harmful to the child. They have such a deep understanding of family life that they know parents and children prosper when bringing up the young becomes less of a strain, they grasp that when others, besides the mother and the father, are involved, the children themselves flourish too. Britain has one of the highest divorce rates in the world, and the number of single parents is rising; young children can place a terrible burden on a couple when so little is done to help the parents, practically, and financially.

Britain now has one of the lowest rates of higher education in the developed world: the young are leaving school without skills, without vocation, without prospects, in increasing numbers. We are told it is a society of choice, but fewer and fewer young people have access to those choices: they have lost their entitlement through a systematic impoverishment of their circumstances, personal and public, from the Poll Tax on 18 year olds living at home, to the running down of the schools.

The Chinese philosopher Mencius based his thought on an idea of fundamental human goodness, and he used this example to prove it: no man, seeing a child playing by a well and about to fall in, would pass by without reaching out for that child. Mencius believed this was a spark in the human spirit that could be fanned into a flame; he also believed that it could be extinguished, and that laws, penalties, and rewards could affect the issue. The Thatcher years have seen many citizens schooled to pass by children on the brink, or even to give them a push; some have been rewarded for it too. If you introduce new measures to save children from the dangers they are running, not only to their health and physical safety, but to their minds and their spirits, you will be staking a claim on the future, and reversing the trend that has made Britain a country to be ashamed of, a place where well-off children can go to a science museum, but the less well off are kept out.

Yours sincerely,

Marina Warner

MARINA WARNER.

Marina Warner is a writer and critic. She has published history, focussing on women's issues and symbolism, books that include *Alone of All Her Sex* and *Monuments and Maidens*, as well as criticism and novels, most recently *The Lost Father*, which was shortlisted for the Booker Prize. In 1989 she published a pamphlet on children, *Into the Dangerous World*, in the Chatto Counter*Blasts* series.

BEN PIMLOTT

London N1.

Dear Prime Minister,

This letter is a personal *cri de coeur*. Alongside your grand schemes, it may sound petty. But it is about an experience that is widely shared, and involves a request which I have heard many other people make. So here goes.

Please could we have some teachers for our children?

I don't care how you do it. You could build better schools. You could free teachers from some of the routine, non-teaching chores they currently have to perform. You could help to raise professional standards and the status of teachers by establishing an autonomous General Teaching Council. You could give schools more money for books, trips and equipment. Above all, you could encourage people to enter teaching by paying those who do more than an unskilled manual wage.

Since, unfortunately, most of these remedies involve spending public money, the real question is where education should come in the pecking order of priorities. My feeling, as a worried parent, is that it has sunk disturbingly low, which is why I am writing this letter.

It is not the first, as a matter of fact, that I have written. Since my children first started to enter the system half-a-dozen years ago, hardly a term has passed without a message flying from my pen to some over-stretched and under-financed official. Since, however, the almost total ineffectiveness of such correspondence has become clear to me, I have begun pitching my barrage higher up. It isn't that I expect more results. It is more that it gives a sense of firing at the right targets.

One letter I wrote a few months after the last election (published in a column I used to write for *The Times*) was addressed to Mr Kenneth Baker, who at the time was pushing through legislation intended to make him the greatest reforming Education Secretary since Rab Butler. In it, I told him about my six-year-old son, who was attending an ILEA-funded primary school in Covent Garden, London.

I explained how, for several months, my son and his classmates had had no teacher: when the Authority advertised the job at the going rate in three national newspapers, not a single qualified person applied. The result (typical, as I understood it, in many London schools) was mayhem: from week to week, even from day to day, the children did not know who they would face each morning, and sometimes there was no teacher at all. When supply teachers were provided, it was a lottery. Some were good. (Antipodean girls doing the grand tour and putting in a few weeks to top up their youth-hostelling money, could be excellent.) Others were almost unemployable. Occasionally the standard was so low it was hilarious. There was the day my son brought home an exercise book in which he had laboriously written a story about Guy Fawkes plotting to blow up James I. Twice the teacher had crossed out 'James' and written 'Charles'.

This, I stressed, was happening not in a sink school in a rough area, or in a strike-torn one run by loony-left staff. On the contrary, it was (and is) a well-run and proud establishment of ancient foundation, efficiently organised on slightly old-fashioned lines. Covent Garden is neither rough nor depressing: a bustling, entrepreneurial, up-and-coming sort of place, it provides a nicely balanced mix of children from business, working-class and ethnic minority families, in one of central London's liveliest communities. There have been no strikes. Despite the school's inadequate Victorian board-school buildings and complete lack of sports facilities (children play on an asphalt roof-top, which turns into a steaming frying-pan in summer), staff morale remains hearteningly – if surprisingly – high.

In short, it is a fine school which – for all its difficulties – offers as big a challenge and opportunity as any in the country. Why then were there no takers? The answer was plain: money. The smallest, meanest, one-bedroom flat anywhere in the capital costs five times the miserable starting salary of a 22 year old with a degree and a postgraduate qualification working in a London primary school. Only a saintly do-gooder with a private income or a high-earning spouse could consider such a job as a long-term proposition.

Mr Baker's radical rhetoric was misdirected, it seemed to me, if it shrugged off this obvious difficulty. Dealing with it was far more important than master plans about the curriculum. 'Like all parents,' I wrote, 'I care what my child is taught and how he is taught it. Yet what matters most is that he should be taught at all.'

Mr Baker did not respond to this plea. But the school fought on, and continues to arouse my admiration. As for my son, a combination of imaginative filling-in by staff, direct parental intervention in the classroom, and private tuition at weekends, have seen him through. But now my wife and I face an identical problem with his younger brother.

You might have thought that a couple of years into the reforms, the crisis would have eased: in fact, it is worse. My second son entered the same school in April 1989 and – four terms later – has so far *never* had a regular teacher. Two supply teachers lasted half a term. Otherwise it has been a kaleidoscope of changing faces. As my son recently put it to me: 'The trouble is, just as you get used to somebody, she goes.'

Our epistolary activities continue. Recently, your Minister of State for Education, Mrs Angela Rumbold, was shown round the school on an official visit, and smiled graciously at the fine display put on by the children and staff. In the hope that such a tour was not just for public show, my wife wrote to her. The reply spoke of her 'concern about the teacher supply position in some parts of inner London' and declared that the Government 'is determined to do what it can to assist'. It spoke, too, of 'several initiatives in hand on teacher recruitment' which 'should make an important contribution to easing the supply problem'.

It added, protectively: 'I am aware that these measures will not resolve the problems overnight.' We wrote back asking how it was that, since the Government had been taking such 'initiatives' for a decade or more, the effects were so hard to discern, and what grounds there were for believing that the latest measures will affect the position before our children complete their education. We are waiting for an answer.

Two children, two letters to ministers: now, with the birth of a new baby this April, I am writing a third in anticipation of a problem which – if the 'initiatives' are all they are cracked up to be – should not arise.

Can you reassure me? And if you do not feel confident that your policies will have had effect by 1995, what do you suggest we do about our third son's schooling? It would be very helpful to be told how he is likely to acquire the skills which you, Mr MacGregor and Mrs Rumbold so frequently tell us are important for Britain in the 21st century, if the schools on offer are reduced to the role of institutional child-minder.

Of course, there is the remedy of paying for teaching outside the state system: we are lucky enough to be able to afford that. But for such a step to be necessary – for this increasingly to have become the resort of a middle class with memories of the heyday of state education – is a terrible indictment. It is also a desperate waste of talent, because of the overwhelming majority of parents and children for whom such an option is not available.

I know that you have plenty of other things on your plate, apart from sorting out my family's problems. But it could be the little things, which to those involved are big ones, that will shape the way voters judge your claim to success. As a parent yourself, you may be able to understand a bit of the frustration we and many thousands of parents like us feel as we observe our bright and eager children who have been told about school, and books, and teachers and learning, and have embarked on the biggest adventure of their childhood with real eagerness – only to confront what frequently amounts to a makeshift arrangement of ushers.

There is, of course, one other possibility: a different government. I doubt, however, that you will share the growing opinion among parents that that is now the only practical alternative.

Yours sincerely,

Ben Pimlott

BEN PIMLOTT.

Ben Pimlott is Professor of Politics and Contemporary History at Birkbeck College (University of London). His books include *Hugh Dalton*, which won the Whitbread Biography Award, and (joint editor with Jean Seaton) *The Media in British Politics*.

David Constantine is a poet, writer, and Fellow in German at the Queen's College, Oxford. He has published a novel, *Davies*, and three poetry collections, including *Watching for Dolphins* (Alice Hunt Bartlett Award) and *Madder* (Poetry Book Society Recommendation and Southern Arts Literature Prize). His *Selected Poems* of Friedrich Hölderlin appeared this year.

DAVID CONSTANTINE

Oxford.

Dear Mrs Thatcher,

Most people never wanted you. Fewer and fewer want you now.
Riots, mass disaffection, beggars on the streets, many thousands
sleeping out, a fifth of the nation stuck in poverty, a large increase
in public ugliness...Will you be handing it on soon to a successor?
To Mr Tebbit, he is the fit person. You made him possible, he
ought to inherit.

I teach. You don't like teachers. I teach in a university. You like
them least of all. But here I shan't be repeating our professional
grievances. I want you to know about something positive you have
done. There is a lot of talk about the demoralisation of teachers, so
perhaps you will be pleased to learn that, as a teacher, I do not feel
at all demoralised and I have many colleagues in the universities
and many good friends in our maligned public sector schools who
do not feel in the least demoralised either. On the contrary, we owe
to you a very clear sense of purpose and responsibility. You are that
against which I have defined my job as a teacher. By 'you' I mean
your convictions, the policies ensuing out of them, your practice
and your tone, and not just yours but also *your* government's – Mr
Tebbit's opinions, say, and the voice of your very loyal Mr Baker –
and not just theirs but your voters' too, the triumphant spirit that
was among them when you were riding highest. Teaching, for
eleven years now, has been an act of contradiction.

Don't get me wrong. I don't teach sociology, nor even history (in
which you have been showing some interest of late). I only teach
literature, poetry especially, and don't be thinking your name is
forever on my lips, it isn't, the contradiction I am speaking of is not
a matter of daily dispute, it is fundamental, it is my basis and my
inspiration. A teacher's subject need not be one easily "politicised"
for his or her teaching to be an act of opposition to you and all your
convictions and all your works.

Should a government be judged according to the *idea* it holds of
what a human being is or might be and of what human society is
and might become? We shall do best, I am sure, not to ask for
anything very special in that way from the governments we elect:
something modest, neutral, not too lofty, not too low either. But
you and your Tory Party have gone abysmally beneath even so

modest a hope or expectation. I wonder when there was last a British Government whose idea of the human being and of human society was as low as yours has been. Perhaps in your history syllabus such questions will be addressed. For what goals and ideals have you put to the people in these eleven years? The lowest, the most selfish, the narrowest, the merely mercantile. You have consistently brought out the worst in people and given it your blessing. We have seen in public office figures and behaviour that previous administrations, Labour or Tory, would have blushed to acknowledge – and seen them cocksure and triumphant. You pitched the message very low, you sanctioned desires and tendencies that people, rightly, used to feel ashamed of.

Teaching literature I am bound to believe that human beings in Britain now are capable of reading things more humane and imaginative and intellectually challenging than the *Sun*. That is why, whatever texts I teach and without ever mentioning you and your colleagues by name, my teaching is necessarily an act of opposition. Education altogether is total and fierce resistance to the notion that fit reading for millions of British people is the *Sun*. Since you have done nothing yourself to counter that notion, and a great deal to encourage it, all teachers *as* teachers, engaged in the education of young people, are your opposition.

You want us to raise standards, and we shall – by opposing what is called Thatcherism: the view of value only as monetary, enterprise only as solitary and self-interested, aspiration only as materialistic, poverty as deserved and contemptible, wealth as proof of virility, and the Kingdom of Heaven as power to dole out charity from on high. Nobody can teach literature and not be, in the whole undertaking, your flat contradiction. Literature widens the imagination and the understanding, it extends compassion, it raises the level of aspiration in personal and social living. Literature, and the teaching of it, become not specifically (about specific issues) ideological, but wholly and intrinsically so by virtue of the ideological context (of your making) in which as teachers we must operate. That is particularly the case in the reading and teaching of poetry. Poetry is, in its very nature, resistant to acquisitive reading, resistant to acquisitiveness; it is *the* anti-commodity, that which refuses to be bought and sold. Poets, when they write, necessarily believe that there is more to life than beggaring their neighbours and brawling for shares in British Gas. Literature denies and opposes you – and again, by 'you' I mean the sort of government you have given your name to and the view of people and society you have done your propaganda for.

And, finally, teaching, whatever the subject, fosters the spirit of criticism. I had a teacher who used to say that the purpose of education is to increase sales-resistance. That will do well enough as a working motto. You have been remarkable chiefly for your unwillingness to tolerate other opinions. To other opinions, when you could not eradicate them, you have offered contempt or, at best, condescension. Necessarily then, in teaching young people to think for themselves, we are teaching a fundamental opposition. What bullies and dubious salesmen have appeared on our television screens in your name! Criticism is a social duty, never more so than in these last eleven years. That is why teachers, however contemptuously you treat them, know that their job is an honourable and necessary one.

I said I was not demoralised, and I'm not. Still, I concede that the drift has been your way for quite some time. Your market ethic is being promoted in the universities now. You have got us evaluating our subjects and our courses in terms of earning power. More graduates go where the money is as quickly as possible. Fewer go into the professions where the money isn't. I concede all that, but emphasise, as contradiction, what has been equally and even more so my experience: the alertness of young people, their generosity, their sense of justice, and their conviction too that the collaborative venture of teaching and learning is, almost by definition, an act of resistance to your divisive and philistine assault.

I always believed that sooner or later a moral revulsion against you would set in. It is happening now. True, some of the outcry is only from people disappointed in the very mean expectations you encouraged them to have. You are failing now even on the level you were aiming at. But more than that I truly believe the revulsion is coming on. Government such as yours is really a belittling of the human being. The *idea* you represented has been an ignoble one. People are more generous, less selfish, more imaginative, more capable of a just society than you ever gave them credit for. How sad and bitter and poor your decade is beginning to look.

Yours sincerely,

David Constantine

DAVID CONSTANTINE.

PENELOPE FITZGERALD

London N6.

Dear Mrs Thatcher,

How disagreeable it is, all this talk about money! You can't, I suppose, have felt this at the beginning of your first term of office, but I am sure that by now you do. All the same, I should like to risk opening the subject again. You remember that you set out on adult life as a chemist. Whether anything disagreeable happened to you then I don't know, but I do know that since that time you have become very reluctant to listen to or even think about scientists.

I am not really asking you a question, but if I were I should expect you to answer, 'I know what is good for people, and I have done as much for British scientists as is good for them.' When, during your first administration, you decided that the share of the national resources assigned to higher education was too large, and must be phased down, the scientists knew they would have to stand at the street-corner and beg like everyone else; of course they would. There was no dispute about their record as Nobel prize-winners, or about their creativeness, or their inventiveness, or their sheer usefulness (it was a British expedition which discovered the hole in the ozone layer). But on the other hand there was no government policy for science because no British government has ever had a policy for science, and they had to use the argument they thought would weigh most with you – that is, the threat of competition. In comparison with France and Germany there was and is a shortfall of £200 million annually in research spending. We train many fewer engineers and technicians than the US, France, Germany or Japan. We file many fewer scientific and technological patents than they do, because we start so many ideas that we cannot afford to develop.

All this is disgracefully true, and yet what the scientists would like to say to you is something quite different. Really they would like to talk, not about competition, but about collaboration. They would like, not to compete, but to collaborate, over, let's say, an AIDS vaccine or an international synchrotron-light source. But you are so reluctant to pay our fair share that, as a recent report puts it, 'we are in serious danger of becoming the lepers of European collaborative science'.

In 1992, then, when scientists will be free to move more or less as they like within careers in the EC countries, who is likely to welcome us? The biologist Sir Peter Medawar (who won the Nobel Prize for medicine in 1960) wrote that 'in no other form of serious creativity is there anything equivalent to a collaboration between scientists, which is a subtle and complex business, because the skill and performance of a team of equals can be more than the sum of individual capabilities'. (He was talking about James Watson and Francis Crick, who, in partnership, interpreted the crystalline structure of DNA.)

Serious creativity, or pure research, shouldn't, so we're often told, be seen as something apart from "near market" research. One thing may lead to the other. But still, everyone knows the difference. Pure, or "non-oriented" research is the expression of the entirely human desire to know. But to know, at the end of the 20th century, costs money. It is this truth, Mrs Thatcher, which, it seems to me, you can't quite bear, and which is at the heart of your hostility to scientists. The hostility, I believe, comes from something other than reason, that is from a series of vivid mental images, stronger than reason itself. Why waste money on science? All Newton needed was an apple,* and all James Watt needed was a steam-kettle. Edison went to work at the age of 12 and never received a grant in his life. Rutherford's team at the Cavendish Laboratory were told to make their own apparatus out of paperclips and string. Alexander Fleming discovered penicillin after a spore floated in by chance through an open window. Brains, luck, hard work, strict economy, keeping a sharp lookout when apples fall or when kettles boil – these were what, in the past, made science cost-effective.

These images, or myths, and others like them, underlie almost everything you do. They are all the more powerful because they are childlike. They have contributed, in the past, to your very real successes. Indeed, you have mythologised yourself. But they are not of much use to you in this particular case. The scientists have remedies to suggest. They wonder whether 48% of their research and development needs to be spent on military projects. They have something to say about the universities, and even more about the

---

* This example comes from Professor J-P Connerade's lecture *Public Perceptions of Science*, given at the Imperial College of Science and Technology, 7 June 1988.

schools. All they need, in the end, is to get you to listen to them quietly for a few minutes. But, disagreeable as it may be, they will have to talk to you about money.

Yours sincerely,

PENELOPE FITZGERALD.

PENELOPE FITZGERALD.

Penelope Fitzgerald is a novelist. Since winning the Booker Prize with *Offshore* in 1979, she has had two other novels on the Booker shortlist, most recently *The Beginning of Spring* (1988). Her youngest child is a research physiologist and reader at University College London, and her political party (Liberal) was 'as far as I can make out, abolished at a stroke while I was out of the room putting on the kettle'.

HANS EYSENCK

Institute of Psychiatry,
University of London.

Dear Mrs Thatcher, Dear Mr Kinnock,

Like most of the voters you address so fulsomely in political party broadcasts and on many other occasions, I am sick to death of the way you introduce political and psychological notions into subjects which are extremely important for our survival as a prosperous and successful nation, but which depend on facts, knowledge, expertise and scientific acumen, rather than the kind of arguments you produce to justify your policies. I have taken as my topic the issue of education, both at school and at university, because this is the only field in which I have any expert knowledge. Looking at what your parties have accomplished in this field, I shudder to think what the future will bring if you continue this suicidal course of mutual recrimination and party political policy formulation! I think most experts would agree that the Labour Party has effectively murdered our previously quite adequate school system, while the Conservatives have equally efficiently stabbed in the back our previously admirable system of university education. All one can say, contemplating this scene of bloody murder, is: 'A plague on both your houses!'

Let us start with Labour, and the killing-off of a very successful tri-partite schooling system, such as still survives very successfully in Germany for instance. Labour introduced a system of comprehensive education, based essentially on unrealistic ideas of equality, a neglect of known facts about genetically determined differences in ability, and the notion that education would be an ideal means for social engineering. The consequences, as Neil Fletcher, the Leader of the Inner London Education Authority, and one of the prime movers of these innovations, has pointed out, is that: 'the Comprehensive dream, in the form we implemented it, has palpably failed. Fewer children from working-class backgrounds are making it to University than in the early-1970s. Romantics, like myself, as a young teacher in the 1960s, believed Comprehensive Schools would achieve an educational revolution through social engineering overnight. We were wrong. Too many inner-city

Comprehensives are no different from the Secondary Moderns in whose premises many are now lodging.'

Mr Fletcher indeed has much to be apologetic about. A recent Report by Her Majesty's Inspectors, not perhaps the most critical of bodies as far as "modern" methods of education are concerned, showed that a third of lessons in our schools are poor, or very poor, and that schools are failing millions of pupils. They have for too long closed their eyes to the major faults of "modern" thinking about our schools. The thinking is disastrously anti-intellectual, with a hatred of competition and a definite scorn for intellectual standards. It embraces a relentless cult of equality and worships a stress-free childhood, totally rejecting the pains and duties of the real adult world. It has failed to oppose absurd notions that streaming and selection are bad, and mixed ability classes are good. It has acquiesced to the silly notion that competitive examinations lead to elitism, that proper grammar, punctuation and spelling make creativity impossible, and that open-plan classrooms, with pupils in groups, are ideal learning conditions. Relaxation and informality are praised, and help in the relentless pursuit of triviality, which takes the place of true learning.

Even the Labour Party officially called into question the results of its own policies, and called for a great debate on these issues. One might have imagined that in this debate factual questions, like the importance of differences in intelligence for educational achievement, and the relevance of selection procedures would play a part; as Mark Snyderman and Stanley Rothman in the book *The IQ Controversy: The Media and Public Policy* have shown, there is virtual unanimity among educational and developmental psychology experts on these issues. Nobody really doubts that intelligence can be reasonably well measured by IQ tests; that intelligence so measured is largely determined by genetic factors; or that intelligence so measured is of vital relevance to educational achievement. But neither the Labour Party nor the Conservative Party has paid any attention to the facts of the case, but have continued a sterile and absurd political debate without any relevance to the real problems of our schools.

Perhaps I am wrong in believing that the politicians are the real villains in the case; an even more promising target is the Civil Service, whose involvement in these matters has been shamefully dishonest, to say the least. Caroline Cox and John Marks, in their book *The Insolence of Office*, have shown how the Civil Service and the Department of Education tried by the most underhand

methods of untrue criticism, leakage of misleading reports, and
suppressio veri to try and give the erroneous impression that the
criticisms Cox and Marks made of the failure of the Comprehensive system, based on very large-scale investigations, were unjusti-
fied. When confronted by the authors of the original report, the
critics had to eat their own words, but the media, unwilling to give
up their ideological left-wing stand, continued to make the same
criticisms, although these had been rejected by their very authors!
All this is ideological warfare, not educational and scientific debate.

These comments are addressed to you, Mr Kinnock. I have not
heard a single word from you to indicate an awareness of the
demonstrated inferiority of British education, as it is now,
compared with German or French education, or the even more
successful Japanese system. Are there any claims to give up the
absurdities of using education for the purpose of social engineering? Is the Labour Party going to pay any attention to established
psychological facts regarding heredity, intelligence and selection?
Are we going to return to intellectually more demanding systems of
teaching and examination? I doubt it, but I am willing to be
reassured.

The harm done by the policies of the Conservative Party during
the past 10 years to our system of tertiary education is hardly less
lethal, as far as our existence as a leading power in the world is
concerned. There has been a failure to support the universities
financially, a failure to establish sufficient tenured places to attract
students to further study, a failure to reward excellence, and a
resounding failure to support research, which is the life blood of all
academic work. As everyone knows, there has been a brain drain of
our best scientific and other talents to the United States, to
Australia and other countries less suicidally inclined. Of course the
Civil Service, with its usual bland incompetence, has tried to deny
this fact by publishing data showing that a number of academics
return to Great Britain, but they simply count heads, rather than
looking at quality. It is usually leading scientists who leave the
country, and it is often the less successful who return. A simple
head count is not a reasonable or rational way of looking at the
matter. It is said that there are lies, damned lies and statistics; I
would rather say that there are lies, damned lies and the kind of
statistics which Civil Servants dish up in order to excuse their
blunders. Such statistics deserve to be taken with more than a grain
of salt; you need a very long spoon to sup with these characters!

The real fault of the Conservative Party has been to extend the principles of short-sighted capitalism to the field of education in general, not heeding the lessons of history that many of the most important scientific discoveries had no obvious economical consequences at the beginning, although later on these became very important. Faraday's work on electricity is an obvious example; many will remember his answer to an old lady who approached him when a very small early model of his newly-invented dynamo was presented to the public. 'What is the use of this toy?' she asked. 'Madam, what is the use of a baby?' he replied. New discoveries of great importance are often made in the pursuit of pure knowledge, without any adumbrations of economic exploitation. To limit scientific research to what is of apparent economic relevance, as the Conservative Government has tried to do, is to kill off much scientific research, including a good deal of the most promising and important. This, indeed, is the sin against the Holy Ghost for which the future will severely punish us. Great Britain simply is no longer a leading member of the scientific community, few budding scientists find the climate congenial or attractive, and in the future we will greatly regret the failures of the Thatcher Government to pay attention to the almost unanimous voices of its academic critics.

I submit that both of you have failed the country by preferring ideological concepts to fact-based views in the matter of primary, secondary and tertiary education. The Labour Party with its absurd insistence on "equality" where there is genetic diversity, and the Conservative Party with its equally absurd insistence on capitalist principles as arbiters of academic performance, have between them made it likely that our future will see a decline in scholastic and academic achievement, a failure to produce the degree of excellence that has always characterised the products of British education, and finally the decline in our living standards which depend to a very large extent on a properly educated, knowledgeable and informed electorate and workforce. Your parties have both let us down drastically over the past twenty years or so, aided and abetted by the Civil Service whose superficial incorruptibility is addled by its demonstrated untrustworthiness and dishonesty. Both parties fail dismally in this examination; that is a solemn truth which the facts compel us to accept, regardless of our voting patterns. In spite of the importance of the facts, and in spite of the warnings originally given in the Black Papers on Education, now so sadly proven correct, there is no improvement in sight, and no interest in these matters even on the part of the smaller parties. If a country has the government it deserves, heaven help Great Britain!

This is a heartfelt message to you two Party Leaders to try and reverse this united march to disaster, to recognise the abysmal failure of your past policies, and to try and remedy, even at this late hour, the evils that your ideological principles have inflicted on our educational system.

Yours sincerely,

HANS J. EYSENCK, Ph.D, D.Sc,
Professor Emeritus of Psychology,
University of London.

Hans J. Eysenck was born in Berlin in 1916, and left Germany as a political protest against the Hitler regime in 1934. After studying in France he went to England and took his Ph.D. in psychology in 1942. He became Professor of Psychology at the Institute of Psychiatry, University of London, in 1955, and retired in 1983. He has written 70 books and 900 scientific articles. His most popular titles include *Check Your Own I.Q.* and *Crime and Personality.*

PAUL DAVIES

Adelaide, Australia.

Dear Mrs Thatcher,

I am writing as a scientist who has recently joined the "brain drain". My decision to move myself and my family to Australia in mid-career was not an easy one. It has involved both financial loss and considerable emotional stress. Nevertheless, I did not feel that I could continue to work in Britain, as part of a system that attaches so little value to basic science. Indeed, it is hard to resist the impression that Britain is deliberately and systematically destroying its science base.

Let me elaborate. Britain has a long and impressive tradition in both the arts and the sciences. Science has always been important to our economy, and it is only right that society should receive some return on its investment in research. However, most of the truly great contributions by British scientists have been made, not as part of a focussed programme of applied research, but in the spirit of "unlocking the secrets of nature".

Volumes have been written about how various discoveries in fundamental, or pure, research have subsequently led to lucrative commercial products. I do not want to dwell on that here. I should like instead to argue that research which is motivated primarily by a desire to *understand* this wonderful universe of ours is a noble and worthwhile pursuit in its own right, and should be supported in any civilised society.

There is a growing attitude in Britain that science is there merely to serve the needs of technology. The notion of science as a *cultural* activity, every bit as important as the arts, is no longer taken seriously. David Davis, Conservative MP for Boothferry, articulated this position when he wrote recently in *The Times* that pure science research is actually 'damaging to Britain because it competes with applied science and technological research'. I am sure that Mr Davis will be delighted that my work on the origin of the universe and black holes is now damaging Australia instead.

I am not arguing that there is anything wrong with applied science and technology. Far from it: a lot of good applied science is under-appreciated in Britain because it is not so glamorous as some fundamental research. But a society that is too mean-spirited to devote some small fraction of its resources to exploring the frontiers *for its own sake* is also a society that stifles creativity. And without human creativity everything suffers, including technology.

I use the term "small fraction" advisedly. One of the more costly pure science ventures that the UK still supports is membership of CERN, the European particle accelerator facility near Geneva. The annual cost of this membership is not a lot more than some people are prepared to pay for a single old master painting.

The threat to British science is not, however, just financial. Most basic research in the UK is done within its universities, and these institutions are under attack on a quite separate front. Your government's passion for changing everything, using funding threats as an incentive, has had a disastrous effect on academic work in both the arts and sciences. The creeping privatisation of British universities is placing research and teaching at the mercy of market forces. Yet these pursuits are long-term investments, too important to be left to the whims and fancy of the market place. Instead of doing the jobs that they have been trained for, more and more expensively educated scientists are frittering away their time designing recruitment posters, planning mail shots, trivialising lecture courses and chasing grants in a desperate attempt to compete for students' and research funds.

It is hard to overemphasise the demoralisation and sense of degeneration which these policies have engendered. It is not so much the changes themselves, disruptive though they are. It is the seemingly endless uncertainty, the impression of muddle, the lack of clear policy direction – let alone understanding – that is so depressing. My period as Professor of Theoretical Physics at the University of Newcastle upon Tyne has coincided almost exactly with your term of office at 10 Downing Street. During that time my former department has shrunk from 30 full-time academic staff to 22, with further cuts probably unavoidable. Up and down the country the pattern is similar. Many of my older colleagues have been forced to retire early, while the bright young physicists have left the country altogether. During the last year or so a national review of physics recommended that up to nearly half of Britain's university physics departments should close because they were becoming too small to be viable – an appalling state of affairs, itself the result of years of under-resourcing. The recommendation was apparently endorsed by the UGC, but that body was itself scrapped the following day, to be replaced by a Funding Council which reaffirmed, then later dropped the recommendation. Since then Britain's university physicists have had to rely on rumour and conjecture to chart the further decline of the subject. How can scientists, who need peace of mind and stability to pursue their abstract work, function properly in this sort of environment?

So who is to blame for this sad state of affairs? I am addressing this letter to you, Mrs Thatcher, because it has been during your term of office that British science has suffered so grievously. The revolution in values brought about by the changes you have initiated have resulted in science becoming marginalised, and scientists being treated as buffoons. In today's Britain, the value of an activity seems to be measured in purely monetary terms.

The trouble is, cultural value cannot be expressed in pounds or dollars. How can one quantify the value of Durham Cathedral, or the works of Shakespeare, or Darwin's theory of evolution? Yet without them we should surely all be the poorer. It is the excitement and drama of basic research that inspires youngsters to seek a career in science, whether or not they end up working at the frontier. Investigating the origin of the universe, or the inner workings of the atom, or unravelling the human genome may or may not lead to marketable products. But if Britain is to deliberately turn its back on such adventurous projects its international prestige as a leader of Western civilisation and culture will never recover.

The sad spiral of demoralisation and decline in British science has gone on for so long that it is beginning to seem irresistible. It is very hard for me to believe that you or your government really care about the plight of British science or British universities, especially those in the north of the country. I spent some years campaigning for British science. Eventually, I came to the conclusion that with your government in power the fight was hopeless. I reluctantly decided to quit and go elsewhere. Fortunately others have stayed behind to carry on the struggle. I hope they'll win before it's too late.

Yours sincerely,

PAUL DAVIES.

Paul Davies is Professor of Mathematical Physics at the University of Adelaide, South Australia. He was until recently Professor of Theoretical Physics at the University of Newcastle upon Tyne, and is well-known as a science populariser. His books include *God and the New Physics* and *The Cosmic Blueprint.* He is a frequent contributor to radio and TV science programmes, and has made a number of highly acclaimed documentaries on topics in fundamental physics, ranging from black holes to the theory of chaos.

SIR ROY SHAW

London N8.

Dear Mrs Thatcher,

I want to write to you about the fate of the arts under your government.

When you came to power, you inherited a tradition nearly 40 years old, one that had been devised in the dark days of World War Two. Government then perceived that the arts are not just a luxury frill, but nourish the spirit of the nation. They were therefore persuaded that the arts should be made much more widely available throughout the land, without sacrificing quality, and provided funds to make that possible. These funds were administered by an independent body, the Council for the Encouragement of Music and the Arts (CEMA), which expressed its aim in the slogan 'The best for the most'. After the War, there was all-party agreement that the scheme had been a great success and should be continued in peace-time. Hence the Arts Council of Great Britain was established, whose tasks are now defined in its Royal Charter as 'to develop and improve the knowledge, understanding and practice of the arts' and 'to increase the accessibility of the arts throughout Great Britain'.

The independence of the Arts Council was promised by what is called 'the arm's length principle', which meant that the government would pay the piper without calling the tune. Some claimed that the principle was a sham and that the Council was just a creature of the government of the day, but I was the Council's chief executive for eight years and knew that they were largely wrong. The independence of the Arts Council was wholly respected during my first four years, when Labour was in power, but during my second four years, when you were in power, that independence was somewhat eroded. One of your arts ministers, for example, dropped the Council's vice-chairman, Richard Hoggart, at a time when his exceptional skills and experience were much prized by the Council. Asked why, the minister could only say 'No. 10 doesn't like him'. In other words, he failed your famous test 'Is he one of us?' That was also the criterion for the appointment of William Rees-Mogg as chairman of the Council and of Luke Rittner as my successor when I retired. The current chairman, Peter Palumbo also made his declaration of Thatcherite faith when you appointed him. I know that no governments appoint their virulent enemies to public office, but before your time no Arts Council chairman made flagrantly party political statements; some of them were Tories, but not your kind of Tory.

The British system of arts funding is admired throughout the world and the main fault in our funding has not been in the system itself, but in the fact that it was for most of the time underfinanced. Never more so than in the past decade, when it has been your policy to hold down the level of public spending. Hence, we spend less than a third (per head of population) of what our main European neighbours spend. When you had been in power three years, an all-party committee of the House of Commons found that the arts were 'irresponsibly' underfunded and in 1990, they still are.

You have had four arts ministers so far, and all have proclaimed that the days when government accepted the main responsibility for arts funding are gone. 'The party's over,' one of them (Lord Gowrie) put it bluntly, before he resigned because he could not live as he wished on a minister's salary. His successor, Richard Luce, has repeatedly warned the arts community not to whinge about the level of government funding, telling them that taxpayers were not keen on public money being used to subsidise the arts. Independent research by the Policy Studies Institute shows that he is quite wrong; the majority want to keep public funding, while a third want it increased.

Ignoring public opinion, your ministers have repeatedly said that the Government's policy was to keep the level of public funding steady, which is a euphemism for keeping it at an irresponsibly low level. The shortfall is to come from business sponsorship, proclaimed by your first arts minister as an idea whose time had come. All your arts ministers have made the boosting of sponsorship their main preoccupation, and they have had some success. And well they might, for business finds sponsorship a very good investment of advertising money. The arts community is much less enthusiastic, though it is so desperately in need of money and so (understandably) afraid of offending sponsors or the Thatcherised Arts Council, that its members rarely dare to speak out against it. True, Lord Rayne, former chairman of the National Theatre confessed that depending on sponsorship was 'a hazardous business' and both the artistic directors of the National and the

Royal Shakespeare Company have criticised the growing influence of sponsors on artistic independence.

Many people think of sponsorship as a form of philanthropy, and are encouraged to do so by conspicuous expressions of gratitude to sponsors in programmes for arts events. However, your arts ministry has frankly stated in a leaflet intended to persuade potential sponsors that sponsorship is not philanthropy, but a commercial deal. Both the Association for Business Sponsorship of the Arts and the Inland Revenue are quite clear that sponsorship is a form of advertising.

However, ABSA has (to its credit) repeatedly said that sponsorship did not exist to relieve the government of its duty to be the main source of arts funding and towards the end of 1989, when leading sponsors began to feel that government was expecting them to bear more of the cost of the arts, they protested and even threatened to withdraw. This was more effective than all the pleas of the arts community in influencing your government which promptly produced some extra funding, though still far less than was needed. As the next election approaches, my guess is that you and your colleagues will produce another small increase in arts funding, aware that it is a cheap way of producing favourable headlines.

However, I trust that the opposition parties (all of them) will make it clear to the electorate that you have consistently starved the arts of adequate funding, have undermined the independence of the Arts Council and of arts organisations. Further, by encouraging sponsors to use the arts for "corporate entertaining" (free seats and champagne) you have introduced a new form of elitism into the arts in place of the original ideal of the best for the most.

Yours sincerely,

Roy Shaw

SIR ROY SHAW.

Sir Roy Shaw was Secretary-General of the Arts Council of Great Britain from 1975 to 1983. Before that, when he was a Professor at Keele University, he acted as advisor to Jennie Lee, Britain's first Arts Minister, and subsequently to her Tory successor, Lord Eccles. In 1987 he published *The Arts and the People*.

TIMOTHY WATERSTONE

Waterstone & Co. Ltd,
London W1.

Dear Prime Minister,

When your Government came to power in 1979, there was an election promise that there would be no candle-end economies in the arts.

I believe that the arts in Britain are uniquely rich in talent, and the level of activity in schools, local art galleries, amateur theatre and drama groups and choirs remains as exuberant as ever. London is proud of its nurturing of five major orchestras; Birmingham, by grace of Simon Rattle's ambition and genius, is building for the nation a further orchestra of international standing; professional theatre throughout the land gives us access to acting standards that are surpassed nowhere; and our flagships – the Royal Shakespeare Company, the National Theatre, the Royal Opera House, and the Royal Ballet – retain glowing international reputations.

But there is a terrible sickness. The RSC's closure of its London programme next winter brought attention to its £3 million deficit, but virtually all the national companies are in similar straits.

The South Bank Centre now shows a deficit of £1.5 million, the Royal Opera House £3.5 million and the major provincial theatres of Leicester, Liverpool, Plymouth and Nottingham are in aggregate deficit of £1.5 million.

Richard Luce – a true man of the 1980s – blames the arts for having 'a welfare state mentality'. Ignoring the efforts of, for example, the ENO, who have increased their income over the last three years by over 50% (to nearly £9 million) and at the same time doubled their sponsorship money. Or the London Philharmonic, whose bold corporate membership scheme, aggressively marketed, now has a lengthy waiting list.

I long for the day when the nation is given political leadership which regards the arts not as a funding burden, but as an opportunity to express to the world the qualities of British life which the world is most ready to admire. The deficits which the arts companies are running are devastating to them but trivial in context of the national genius they encapsulate and express.

The penny-pinching is mean-spirited and undignified. The Arts Council receives now £175 million per annum from Government to distribute nationwide, and the Council's grants for the two following years – adding 3.5% and 3.0% – will be considerably below the rate of inflation.

The one thing the current Government hates above all else is whingeing from arts companies that are recipients of "hand-outs" from the national purse, but the sums are simply too low, the aspiration too hopelessly limited, the damage done grave beyond measure. The RSC and the National may be able to look for profitable West End transfers, but so few have this safety net. Northern Ballet bravely drives for more sponsorship, Manchester City Council determinedly relaunches the Hallé, and Birmingham – such a proactive force now – has, as well as the CBSO, its Repertory Theatre that is doing such positive things to maintain its standards whilst holding its financial equilibrium.

Birmingham is trying hard to start forging links with Europe, looking to learn from Liverpool no doubt where the national museums and galleries on Merseyside have adopted such a pro-European stance. They are finding their rewards and too few British arts organisations are following them in their European zeal.

Much funding is available from across the Channel – Merseyside has, for example, received a £5 million grant from the European Regional Fund – and any British artist or group will be able to receive grants from any European city in which they perform.

And here lies the point; there is a huge difference in the amount of money spent on culture in most of Europe in comparison with Britain's lamentable government backing.

Germany spends £1.7 billion on the arts, France £2 billion, Italy £1.9 billion, while Britain spends just £700 million.

The reaction of the Minister to the Wilding Report on Arts Funding was apocalyptic. The Report looked for a shift in responsibility for funding from the Arts Council to regional arts boards, and this in itself was a line of thought that has much to recommend it, with the responsibility for the funding and development of star companies located provincially best handled by that region's arts association.

The Minister's reaction, however, was to strip the Arts Council down to simply an advisory body regionally, with executive control only over the blue-chip big five (the Royal Opera House, the Royal Shakespeare Company, the National Theatre, the English National Opera and the South Bank Centre) and little else.

The Arts Council thereby becomes both too strong and too weak – its centre now wholly London-based gives it an artificially metropolitan lobbying base, yet its regional leadership dissolves into a flabby rubber-stamping role.

The Arts Council has often been an irritant to us all – overly bureaucratic, and irresponsible in its peripheral activities (who can forget the Arts Council shop in Long Acre?). Yet it's an institution which has been a great source of strength and influence in its 40 years of life. It was born under Attlee at a time when the nation, exhausted by the War, clung to the hope that cultural riches belonged equally to us all. In its life, the Council has genuinely held firm for national standards of excellence in the arts, has boldly promoted initiatives (black theatre, and avant-garde art) that desperately needed sustenance, and has overall been the envy of other civilised nations that lacked co-ordinated arts leadership of the sort the Arts Council provides.

We can accept with enthusiasm the recommendations of the Wilding Report that envisaged devolution to the regions of funding control of perhaps 75% of arts companies, but I view with dismay the prospect of a diminished Council and the prospect of cultural leadership dispersing and disintegrating.

I want to see an Arts Council rise from the ashes of the 1980s to a bold new future of massive funding for culture and exhilarating and proactive political support from No. 10 itself. The pettifogging deficits that are crippling our magnificent arts companies should be eliminated in one bold sweep, the RSC's winter season restored, the Liverpool Philharmonic properly funded, the Northern Ballet put firmly on its feet, Kent Opera resuscitated. If Italy can allocate £1.9 billion to its nation's arts groups then so can we. I long for political leadership that believes in the nation's culture, and wants to show it to the world.

Yours sincerely,

TIMOTHY WATERSTONE.

Timothy Waterstone is a bookseller and businessman, the founder and Chairman of the bookselling chain Waterstone & Co Ltd, co-founder and Deputy Chairman of the publisher Sinclair-Stevenson Ltd, and Chairman of Priory Investments Ltd. He has served on the management committee of the Booker Prize since 1985, and is a director of the London Philharmonic Orchestra and the Academy of Ancient Music.

JOHN CALDER

John Calder (Publishers) Ltd,
London WC2.

Dear Mrs Thatcher, Dear Mr Kinnock,

I am writing to you both about a subject in which neither of you has expressed very much personal interest, the position of the arts in the UK. It is clear that you, Mrs T, see the arts as a fad that some people seem to want, God knows why as they never seem to make any money except for a few rock singers who are never 'one of us', as you put it. You are willing to tolerate them within limits as long as the beneficiaries pay for their fad or can find sponsors to do so. You also think the arts may be subversive, as with *The Falklands' Sound*, so you would rather they were expensive enough to suit the rich, giving harmless pleasure without too many ideas. As ideas flourish in universities, you have done what you can to reduce that danger and encourage institutes of higher learning to inculcate greed and cunning in the young, rather than teaching them to use their minds for other purposes, such as the improvement of society.

You, Mr K, are probably fairly amiable towards the arts in your woolly way, but you do not want to lose any votes by actually having a policy, and you suspect they are probably irrelevant except to the rich and a few oddball socialists like Norman Buchan, who you fired for actually wanting to do something about them.

You have both missed the boat. The arts are what separate us from dumb animals: our entire human progress from before the Stone Age is due to them. They are as necessary as food and shelter; they give life its flavour and tell us whether we are living in a good or a bad society. The need becomes obvious when we are starved of them and the change of perception of the whole country, reflected in current opinion polls, is largely caused by the arts becoming grim and hungry, reflecting the state of the country. People are thinking in a new way because they do not have the plush cosy omnipresence of the arts that Jennie Lee made, perhaps, too easily available. Art is communicated in new ways, not least through popular forms, but also in poetry, drama, the novel, as well as the visual and musical arts. They have gone to some extent underground as they did in Eastern Europe for so many years, but they were working there all the time, waiting their time. Who is President of Czechoslovakia now? Why, a writer: Havel – a man who could describe what was wrong.

Art will always find a way. When the arts become poor they find new ways to bite. What you have failed to realise, Mr T, is that the artist is no saint and can be bought like most other people (not all artists, of course), and if subsidised and given an easy time, they often become good Conservatives and never bite the hand that feeds: Macmillan and Heath knew this, but then to them art was part of the good life, which Conservatives used to argue they could provide better than Labour could. You do not meet Conservative artists these days.

Mr K, you have a great opportunity just now if you could bring yourself to suggest that you believe in Art and want it to be a part of everyone's life and of the educational system. It is the artists who are saying that perhaps someone in your party could suggest that more convincingly than you do, thereby increasing Labour's election chances. Right now you have no positive image. Could it be because, unlike Healey, Foot, John Smith and others, you have never given much evidence of having the kind of thinking mind that is sharpened by contact with the arts? But I am sure that both of you think you know best, and would rather listen to your own certainties than to what is being said in the country. How lucky you both are that none of the other parties has an arts policy either.

Yours sincerely,

JL Cll

JOHN CALDER.

John Calder is a publisher and editor of modern literature. He went to school in England and Canada, and studied political economy at Zurich University. His pioneering and vitally important work in publishing and promoting new and experimental writing, and in particular contemporary French and American novels, has been an example to less imaginative British publishers for 40 years. He has been Managing Director of John Calder (Publishers) Ltd since 1950, and has edited many publications, including *A Samuel Beckett Reader*, *Henry Miller Reader* and *William Burroughs Reader*.

TESSA BLACKSTONE

Birkbeck College,
University of London.

Dear Mrs Thatcher,

Earlier this year I sent your ministerial colleagues in the Home Office a copy of the Counter*Blast* I wrote on Prisons and Penal Reform for the Chatto and Windus series. I failed to send you one too; this was an omission. It has denied me the pleasure of being able to say 'I told you so', since the public's response to the recent prison riots is completely consistent with what I said in the pamphlet. In spite of what you may have thought, public opinion is more liberal and humane than the views espoused by the *Sun*. Most people think far too many people are sent to prison. They think there are more effective and more humane ways of dealing with all but the most serious offenders. Anyway perhaps it is just as well I did not send you a copy, as it now gives me the opportunity to set out the arguments in a letter, after the worst prison riots for many years, which must give you as much cause for concern as the rest of us.

Riots in prisons are terrifying events. They can lead to many innocent victims amongst staff and inmates, who may be physically injured or psychologically scarred or both. Damage to property may be considerable. Above all they pose appalling dilemmas for the authorities as to how to restore order. There is nothing whatsoever to say about them as events in themselves which is positive. Yet if what took place in a number of British prisons in April 1990 turned out to have been a turning-point in our views about how to handle convicted offenders, they will have been a catalyst for which we can be grateful. If on the other hand as soon as the immediate problems they pose are resolved we fall back into resignation and inactivity with respect to our appalling penal system, it will only be a matter of time before more riots take place. Meanwhile a great political opportunity to do something will have been wasted. Moreover, you, Mrs Thatcher, will not have got to grips with a serious failure of public policy where Britain's record is deplorable compared with most of our European neighbours. You will have had between 12 and 13 years to do so. Time is running out, but enough remains if you act now. If you do so the history books will record your courage in tackling a tough problem. If you do not, the judgement will be that your Government did little more than throw money at the problem – behaviour you have always deplored.

You must be asking yourself a number of questions. First, why are we spending so much money on a penal policy which is so singularly unsuccessful? Why do we rely so heavily on a form of punishment which is so costly to the society at large and to the individual concerned? Why have the various alternatives made so little impact on the number in prison? Why are the conditions in our prisons such a disgrace?

Most of those convicted of indictable offences should be given non-custodial sentences. Imprisonment is unlikely to help them mend their ways. Incarceration with those who have committed more serious crimes is a good training ground for committing further crime on release. Long days of enforced idleness, inactivity and dependence is a very poor preparation for greater social responsibility and self-reliance on release. It costs between £300 and £500 to keep a person in prison for a week. Non-custodial alternatives are far cheaper. For example it costs as much to keep a young person in prison for 2½ weeks as it does to place him on a Community Service Order for a year; and it costs as much to keep an adult in a local prison for 3½ weeks as it does to supervise him on probation for a year. Yet the proportion of offenders who are imprisoned has increased substantially during your years as Prime Minister; 21% of adult men and 8% of adult women convicted of indictable offences are now sent to prison, compared with 17% and 3% a decade ago. Moreover, little has been done by your Government to deal with the grotesque disparities in sentencing practices of courts in different parts of the country.

The key to the problem is sentencing policy. However difficult it may be to persuade judges and magistrates to give up some of their discretion, this must be done. The recent White Paper which sets out ways of reducing the numbers in prison is a step in the right direction. However it fails to get to grips with the problem of how to introduce a coherent sentencing policy with statutory guidelines for magistrates and judges. Without a fundamental change of this sort, it is doubtful whether your proposals will crack the problem of too many people in prison.

To invest large sums of money in building more prisons is folly. Millions of pounds will go down the drain on creating yet more inhumane institutions. Our objective should be to halve the number of people in prisons over the next five to ten years. If this were accepted we could close those prisons with the worst buildings and would not need an expensive prison building programme. New prisons mean improved physical conditions and getting rid of the disgusting practice of slopping out, but do little or nothing to improve regimes in other respects. There are new penal institutions which are still locking up young men for 23 hours a day. The money would be much better spent on improving some existing prisons and expanding non-custodial ways of dealing with offenders. Prisons should be confined to those who commit the most serious crimes and to violent offenders from whom society must be protected.

Yours sincerely,

Tessa Blackstone [signature]

TESSA BLACKSTONE.

Baroness Tessa Blackstone is Master of Birkbeck College. She is a writer, educationalist, political advisor, and a Labour member of the House of Lords. Her previous posts have included Deputy Education Officer (Resources) at the Inner London Education Authority, and Professor of Educational Administration at the University of London Institute of Education, and she was a member of the Central Policy Review Staff in the Cabinet Office during the Wilson and Callaghan administrations. Her latest book is *Prisons and Penal Reform* (Chatto Counter*Blasts*, 1990).

Vivien Stern has been director of NACRO (National Association for the Care and Resettlement of Offenders) since 1977. Before then she worked in education, and subsequently race relations. She is the author of *Bricks of Shame: Britain's Deprived Prisons* (1987), *Imprisoned by Our Prisons* (1989), and most recently *Deprived of Their Liberty* (1990), a study of Caribbean prisons.
    NACRO is the principal non-governmental organisation in the offender field in England and Wales. As well as promoting the care and resettlement of ex-offenders within the community and community involvement in crime prevention, NACRO provides research, information and training services for those interested in or who work within the criminal justice system.

VIVIEN STERN

NACRO,
London SW9.

Dear Mrs Thatcher,

I don't imagine you think very often about prisons. I don't blame you. It is not a cheerful subject and there is not a lot to gain, you may feel, by trying to sort them out. But I would urge you to do so.

Our prison system is a monstrous leftover from an earlier age. When you walk into one of our old Victorian prisons you feel you are stepping back into another century. The bare grey walls, the little dungeon-like windows, the prison officers in uniforms signifying a bygone notion of authority, the gruesome humiliating rituals, such as slopping out.

We hear a lot about slopping out, but without experiencing it I wonder if it is possible to imagine the feeling of gradual degradation induced by having to use a bucket in front of one or two others, live in a small room with it for perhaps 11 hours and then queue up carefully carrying this full bucket, waiting to empty it in an overflowing sewage system.

So you have a problem of bad buildings, and it is made worse because you have too many prisoners. Even if prisons were not overcrowded you would have too many prisoners because we seem to be a country with a great hunger for punishment and our punishment hunger leads us to lock up more of our citizens in proportion than any other country in western Europe – and with the big reductions underway in eastern Europe we shall probably soon have overtaken them too. Why this is so is complex. But it does us no good. We lock up more. We lock them up younger, and they come out worse, more criminally sophisticated, bitter and often brutalised. And we lock up a disproportionate number of black people. Not surprisingly the racism in the wider society and in criminal justice leads to a prison population where 15½% are black compared with 4.4% of the population.

So we lock up too many in terrible conditions. But that is not all that is wrong. Our attitude to our prisoners is deeply punitive. We want them to know that they are at the bottom, that we hate them and despise them. An English prisoner who had experienced both the English and the Dutch systems said that in Holland 'they treat you like a human being. They say "enjoy your meal", "good morning"...I just can't believe that they don't despise you because you are a criminal. In England they punish you for being a criminal. Then they punish you while they're punishing you. Then you're punished for the rest of your life.'

We have many ways of showing our prisoners we despise them, the horrible buildings no one bothers to brighten up, the reception procedures, stripping and reducing the prisoner to anonymity, the issuing of numbers and knowing prisoners by their number thereafter, the tatty visiting-rooms where the spouses and families are allowed in after a long wait in the street in the rain, the issuing of ill-fitting regulation clothes to male prisoners and the frequent failure to provide clean clothes even once a week. And women prisoners do no better. They may wear their own clothes but the petty restrictions and the humiliations are still there.

All this is not the fault of the prison officers. They work there. They would prefer to work somewhere clean, hygienic and interesting. They would rather do something worthwhile and go home at the end of the day feeling they had succeeded in something. And they often try to humanise a basically uncaring system. But they get little training and scant opportunity to do a better job in a system that is constructed, conceived and run like ours.

Who gains from having a system like this? Absolutely nobody. Not prison staff, prisoners, society – or the politicians. Because there is always trouble. In April 1986 there were flare-ups and riots in 40 prisons. In October 1986 Risley remand centre saw trouble. In March 1988 there was a disturbance at Bedford prison. In May 1988 there was trouble at Rollestone temporary prison. In the summer of 1988 there was trouble at Haverigg and Hindley and at Lindholme. In April 1989 Risley remand centre was the scene of further riots. And in April 1990 we saw trouble in 15 prisons and the spectacle of Strangeways, that monument to Victorian penology, where a dedicated governor and staff were trying to do the impossible, slowly being destroyed before the TV cameras of the world.

No one wants our system to be like this. So let's change it. What should we do? We could start with the Prison Service's own mission statement (as it is called) engraved on an aluminium plate and stuck up in every prison as well as reproduced in every Prison Service document. It says 'It is our duty to look after them [prisoners] with humanity'. If we started there – and went through every ritual and routine that prisoners endure, subjecting it to the 'humanity' test and changing whatever failed the test, we should already have a totally different prison system, less brutalising for staff and prisoners alike. Such a change would inevitably mean a new approach to contacts with the outside world. The statutory minimum of a half hour's visit every four weeks would be increased. There would be access to telephones for all prisoners in some way or other, unlimited letter-writing opportunities and much more home leave.

Having created a more humane framework we must then take advantage of the new atmosphere to introduce a range of constructive activities in prison that fill the prisoners' day and seem to them to lead somewhere – to a job, a new skill, maybe just to developing a potential for learning, writing or art.

In the meantime the work must be done to establish a legal framework for imprisonment. One of the major reasons for the pressure-cooker state of the prisons is that prisoners have so few legal channels of redress. Practically anything that happens to a prisoner in prison is at the Home Secretary's discretion. And the major channel of complaint is to...the Home Secretary.

Finally, let us stop sending so many people to prison. Your Government knows it does no good. A recent government publication said, characteristically, that prison may simply serve 'to make bad people worse'. Let us tackle the racism in the criminal justice system, so that the shamefully high proportion of black prisoners is reduced. Let us stop sending children under 18 to prison establishments at all. Prison is no place for them. Let us realise that a high prison population does not reduce crime. It probably increases it. And for those that do go to prison, let it be a place that may not make anyone better but can at least not make them worse.

Yours sincerely,

VIVIEN STERN.

JULIAN MITCHELL

Llanvaches,
Newport, Gwent.

Dear Mrs Thatcher, Dear Mr Kinnock,

Under British parliamentary democracy the rough justice of majority rule is acceptable only so long as the overall system is seen as generally fair. We win some, we lose some. Once that general sense of fairness is lost, our society is in serious trouble. Several recent cases have revealed an unacceptable amount of injustice in British justice, a flaw at the heart of the system.

I'm not concerned with the obvious public dissatisfaction with the trustworthiness of the police, though God knows that needs immediate attention, so much as with the trustworthiness of our judiciary. Not that I think our judges are corrupt; all the ones I've ever known have been scrupulously honest and honourable men, in their own terms. But those terms need re-examination.

The exclusiveness of the legal profession has been a source of bitterness for centuries, and it's not simply a matter of its narrow social base. Anyone from any social background who enters the law becomes a lawyer; that is, adopts a very narrow and limited view of his job. And the longer he or she stays in the law, the narrower and more limited the view becomes. By the time people become judges, their experience has largely unfitted them for dealing with ordinary human life.

The very language of the law is incomprehensible to most people. It seems deliberately concocted to make them feel stupid. And the procedures are equally baffling. The delays – the law's delays have been the subject of satire since law began. But what's funny about keeping a prisoner on remand for months or years without trial? What's funny about being kept hanging about for justice, while lawyers grow rich by procrastination?

But the most scandalous form of delay, the one which has brought most distrust of our system in recent years, is the delay in redressing injustice. And here you, as politicians, are as much to blame as the lawyers. There have been too many truly shameful cases where government enquiries seem to have gone to elaborate lengths to disguise the truth of injustice in order to protect the majesty of the law and the face of the ruling establishment. This is a great wrong. When politicians collude with judges they are going against the whole principle of the separation of powers. If the politicians won't judge the judges, who will? As with the police, self-policing has manifestly failed to satisfy public feeling.

For the law is quite majestic enough to need no extra protection. It dresses ordinary people in solemn gowns and ponderous wigs to hide their ordinary human capacity for error, while the unjustly sentenced are stripped of all but the bare necessities. The judge returns from the court over which he reigns to lavish chambers, provided by the state, while the unjustly sentenced is shoved in a filthy and overcrowded cell with disgusting sanitation. The judge's power is continually enhanced by servants both legal and domestic, while the state removes all power from the unjustly sentenced. He does not even retain the right to protest, for protest in our prisons is met by physical beating and extension of his sentence.

Society must, of course, be protected, from the wicked and dangerous. But no one seriously believes any longer that imprisonment can reform or even improve most prisoners. It is sad, but something all societies come to in the end: some people simply have to be locked away, in prisons or mental homes, or a combination of both. But because the loss of freedom is the loss of something so basic to human nature, it is absolutely vital that as soon as there is any question of wrongful imprisonment or miscarriage of justice or "sectioning" under the Mental Health Act, it should be investigated at once. And that no one's reputation, no one's face, no one's feelings should be spared to make sure that wrong is swiftly put right.

Now I'm sure that most lawyers think that that is more or less what happens now: which shows how out of touch they are. They have a horrible phrase: 'hard cases make bad law'. This means that it is better that injustice should sometimes be done than that the judgements of one of their own should be questioned. Questioning a judgement, after it's been through the interminable system of appeal (and yes, I do know some countries are even more tortuous than we are, but what has that to do with the justice of British justice?) is felt somehow to question the whole fabric of solicitors and barristers and Inns of Court and gowns and wigs and the place of the Lord Chancellor in the grand hierarchy of the state. Because the judiciary, when it comes down to it, is as jealous of its position and careful for its self-importance as any city corporation. And as easily frit. Because of this failure of nerve, this failure to see beyond the needs of the law to the larger needs of society, the law fails us all. Justice is all too often not only not done, it is seen to be not done. When the truth comes out, fifteen years later, a lifetime later, justice seems a dishonourable word used by a privileged caste to protect its privilege. And the sense of fairness on which our system depends is gravely threatened.

So what I want, you two, is swifter justice, and swifter redress of injustice and admission of error. The closing of ranks by governments and judges to conceal the truth can never be in the interest of society in the long run, whatever the short-term benefits.

Let our prisons and mental hospitals be places where people can have some basic human rights and dignities. Deprivation of liberty is punishment enough; by degrading people further, we degrade ourselves. And above all let them be places from which people wrongly condemned can get out as soon as possible.

If you can arrange that, I'll vote for you. Perhaps.

Yours sincerely,

Julian Mitchell

JULIAN MITCHELL.

Julian Mitchell is the son and grandson of lawyers. He writes for stage, films and TV. His best-known play is *Another Country*, which deals with one form of injustice and its results. His most recent television has dealt with law and justice through the conscience of *Inspector Morse*.

Jeanette Winterson is a novelist. She won the Whitbread Prize first novel award for *Oranges Are Not the Only Fruit*, which was recently shown on television. Her other books are *The Passion*, winner of the John Llewellyn Rhys Prize, *Boating for Beginners*, and *Sexing the Cherry*.

JEANETTE WINTERSON

London NW5.

Dear Mrs Thatcher,

Is it the duty of Government to legislate on love? It is certain that although love can be controlled by an Act of Parliament, it cannot be encouraged. Governments can limit the supply of love but they cannot increase it.

In 1988 your Government decided to try and limit love. You recognised that love, being true to its ebullient self, was not simply to be found in the four square walls of heterosexuality, it was out on the street, blooming in the garden, and sometimes, because its roots were strong, it threatened the four square walls themselves. A few houses fell down.

The love that dare not speak its name had begun to sing; its siren song of humanity and diversity and celebration was freeing large numbers of men and women from guilt and persuading others that an authentic choice, based on feeling, not convention, was the only dignified way to live. Those who were not directly affected found that a new atmosphere of understanding created a proper arena for debate. Sexuality could at last be discussed not in terms of pathology or normality but in terms of men and women and love.

Everyone, regardless of their sexual persuasion, stood to profit from this. A rigid society is a vulnerable society; it accumulates fear and it breeds unrest. It forces revolt because it refuses any other reason but its own. It suffocates in technicalities and red tape. Its citizens must be told how to think and what to think. Our society, whilst intoning its commitment to choice and to privacy, made it legal to follow some of its citizens to their bedroom door.

Section 28 of the Local Government Act was designed to make homophobia acceptable again. First and foremost, it intended to discourage homosexuality, to take it out of the realm of choice and back into wilful perversion. Secondly, it determined to tell everybody what was normal; especially children. Children and young adults were not to think that they could be happy and fulfilled outside of a heterosexual context. They were not to imagine that real family life was possible for lesbian and gay couples. 'Pretended family relationship' was the most hateful phrase in all of that petty and hateful piece of legislation.

Your Government, never hallmarked by its powers of imagination, found it impossible to see past the Cornflake adverts. Applied personally they meant that I, Jeanette Winterson, if married to the most revolting man in England and bringing up a child in whatever circumstances, would be participating in a proper family relationship. If I, Jeanette Winterson, chose to care for a child along with my girlfriend, who is successful, stable, and like me, happy, we would all be pretending. Quality of life means nothing when taboos are at stake.

I remember being in the House of Lords when Lord Caithness was warning his fellow peers, most of whom were fast asleep, that if children were not protected from homosexual propaganda, any number of them might become homosexuals themselves. That would be terrible wouldn't it, when instead they could sacrifice themselves and their partners to an emotional and sexual wilderness? Why be happy when you could be normal?

Section 28 has bitten a few times since it was implemented: the case of the schoolchildren being refused a production of Britten's *Death in Venice*; the two women teachers who were suspended because they were thought to be having an affair; Essex County Council trying hard to stop any gay group meeting on its premises. There are others and they are bad enough but they are nothing compared to the climate of intimidation and fear the Act has created.

What is it that your Government is afraid of? You are afraid of love. Love in marriage is relatively safe; it can be and usually is, tied to economic factors. It is bounded by convention, hedged and ditched with propaganda from Mills and Boon, through pornography to our ubiquitous Cornflake advert. It can be controlled.

Those outside of any system tend to be the most critical of it, the ones most alive to its injustices. If homosexuality were allowed to flower, at its own rate, alongside heterosexuality, then I suspect that the institution of marriage, the nuclear family, that basic unit of social control, would have to change. It could not, as it does now, favour the man, and it could not, as it does now, claim a monopoly on love. Love in its diversity would encourage many different ways of being together, many different ways of bringing up a family. One of those ways might be marriage. None of them would be pretend.

Yours sincerely,

Jeanette Winterson

JEANETTE WINTERSON.

MARGARET DRABBLE

London NW3.

Dear Mrs Thatcher,

There are many topics on which I could not very usefully address you, but let me confine myself to one on which I believe we are in some sympathy. You have yourself on several occasions expressed your disgust at the state of British streets, open spaces, and motor verges, and have admitted that they bear poor witness to our country internationally and do no good to our tourist industry. What must visitors think as they survey the garbage in the West End, the poor standards of some of our motorway and transport cafés, the broken paving stones and unswept pavements, the non-functioning escalators of the Underground, the graffiti-daubed bus stops and beggar-haunted bus stations? They are not very pleasant for us locals either. I know you do not like this any more than I do, for when you were in Singapore you went out of your way to visit and praise the cleanliness of the subway and public transport system. If you were to travel on the tube or the buses or the commuter trains in Britain, you would find the contrast even more shocking.

Other great cities are not as dirty as London. This is not because their citizens are tidier and more public-spirited than we are, but because their administrators spend more money on cleaning them up. You quite rightly pointed out that one of the by-products of an affluent society is rubbish (fast food cartons, drinks cans, bottles, throwaway goods of every kind) but surely an affluent society can afford to dispose of its own garbage? Market forces will not remove it by magic: legislation and incentives are needed. Educating children in the ways of cleanliness may help, but it will not alone remove the problem, as mothers who spend their lives wiping sticky surfaces and picking up plastic toys know all too well. Human beings have a natural tendency to throw things on the street, and the more we have to throw the dirtier the streets become, and the less people feel the obligation to carry rubbish home or look for a bin.

Anyway, it is not only a question of litter. There is also the question of grime, decay, pollution, ageing. I will not embark here on the larger Green debate, the environment debate, but will confine myself to the domestic and the municipal. You claim to be a good and thrifty housewife, and have been somewhat unfairly teased for this. A good housewife knows that a property needs regular maintenance, inside and out. Money must be spent on paint, brickwork, drains, repairs, plumbing, garden upkeep. Some of this expenditure shows and gains neighbourly admiration and credit, but some does not. But its absence, over a prolonged period, shows increasingly, and the property that is not maintained decays and loses value. Much of Britain is now extremely shabby. I know this because I like to wander around it, and unlike Prime Ministers and Royalty I go to places that have not been cleaned up in anticipation of my arrival.

I was in Sheffield last month. Sheffield is the fifth largest city in Britain. You have visited it once only in your ten years of power, or so I am told. Anyway, that is what its inhabitants believe. It is a city that has been through and survived deep recession. It has fought back against the collapse of the steel industry, soaring unemployment, sectarian strife, and the partly accidental fall-out from the Miners' Strike. Now it is in good heart again. It has attracted new jobs and the World Student Games 1991. But it bears some visible scars. You should take a stroll round some of the older council estates. True, some have bought and done up their council houses, and that is good. But what of those who cannot afford to do so, and for whom the Council can provide no new housing? Do you know what conditions people are living in? And these are not even the worst parts of the country. I think you might be shocked by some of the housing in affluent Britain.

It is quite easy to stay in the nice parts and think everything is going well. At times the West End and the City and the county towns and villages look wonderful. But try the Northern Line, not even in rush hour. Wander past the grid-protected shops of dismal estates. Go down a pedestrian underpass or two. I'm not even speaking of the possibility of meeting a tramp in a cardboard box – just of the puddles of dirty water, the dank stained cement, the paper bags, the old shoes and shoulder pads.

I would like to recommend that all Cabinet Ministers should take an unannounced and if possible incognito trip on public transport at least once a month. And it would be good if they were encouraged to wander on foot round some of the less picturesque corners of our towns and cities. Then go and have a look at Paris, or Geneva, or Venice, or Harare, or Toronto. Cities don't just spontaneously tidy themselves up. They need money, effort and, dare I say it, planning.

Queen Victoria, when she travelled in the industrial North, was so appalled by the dirt and squalor that she asked to have her carriage windows blinded. We laugh at her for that now.

Please, Mrs Thatcher, go to Sheffield, and wander round both the nice bits and the not-so-nice bits. People would be pleased to see you there. They'd be pleased to see you in the Mozart Estate in Kilburn. People are always very pleased to see Michael Foot on the 24 bus, whether they vote for him or not. Go on, give it a try.

Yours sincerely,

MARGARET DRABBLE.

Margaret Drabble is a novelist and critic, born in Sheffield in 1939. Her latest novel, *A Natural Curiosity* (1989) is a sequel to *The Radiant Way* (1987), and she is currently struggling with the third part of this unplanned trilogy. She edited the *Oxford Companion to English Literature*, and is now working on a Chatto Counter*Blast* pamphlet on housing and mortgage interest tax relief. She is a member of Charter 88.

DAVID ASTOR

Milton under Wychwood,
Oxfordshire.

Dear Mrs Thatcher,

One of the achievements that few would deny you is a rekindling of our national pride. But what comprises this self respect, this national identity: more than guns and GDP?

Britain is a beautiful country. Pride in the beauty of our islands is a characteristic of our race.

For millions of our compatriots it is a source of immense emotional satisfaction to know that the British countryside surrounds the cities and towns in which they work. It rests there as a source of peace and relaxation, softening the harshness of commerce and infrastructure yet working to feed the nation following its timeless duty. They feel this though they own no land, nor hope to do so. They love their Britain, their countryside.

I find it odd that you, who have often been able to identify the older instincts of your country with great precision, appear to lack an insight into this aspect of our culture.

I say this because, during your eleven years as Prime Minister, you have not come across as being very interested in the countryside. When you speak of environmental issues they have nearly always been global ones, as if there were no real threat to our own countryside. We hear of "rural development" but it is only commercial enterprise that you seem to have in mind. Your Government, so resolute on foreign affairs, economic and social policy, dithers for consensus when faced with the destruction of our rural heritage. The overwhelming theme of your message to the farming industry in your eleven years is that it must "diversify".

Your steps actually to pay farmers for some of the environmental benefits have been small-scale and hesitant. As a result, too many farmers have, in effect, been encouraged to move out of farming, to become more like real people in cities, by making their farms more like factories and suburbia.

Yet for all this government inertia, colossal changes to the countryside have been set in train by a combination of unswerving agricultural policies and technological advance. Some of this is inevitable, and some can be blamed on the EC, but by no means all.

We have come to the point where we produce far more food than we can consume domestically or sell abroad without huge subsidy. This has led to a series of wild estimates about the existence of large areas of "surplus land", the size of several counties, no longer needed to grow food.

So the farm pundits argue that the future for Britain lies in taking vast areas out of production so that the remaining arable farmers of the east can make fat profits based on the subsidised lunacy of high CAP food prices.

Intensify! Intensify! they call. Pour on more chemicals. Nothing must get in the way of super efficient modern agriculture. Thus Norfolk, Suffolk and much of South East and Central England are destined to become sanitised, disinfected, regimented food production factories. Poorer arable land will be "set-aside", taken out of agriculture. Huge swathes of England will be left to purposelessly grow weeds, ripening to become the developer's plum site.

Far from being a way of re-creating lost landscapes and wildlife habitats, this land will be chosen on a farmer's whim, public money will be used where the farmer wants, not where conservation suggests.

If we are lucky, Cornwall, Cumbria and Cymru, will grow sheep, but soon sheep too will be in surplus, at the cost of denuded hillsides and eradicated heather and we will need set-aside in the hills.

So what are the alternatives to letting the countryside polarise into highly intensive areas and set-aside ones? It is beyond dispute that if we continue to grow as much food as we do per hectare of land then we shall have surpluses. But remember that surpluses are entirely artificial, the equivalent of British Leyland producing stockpiles of subsidised cars no one wants to buy. Without huge subsidies there would be no surplus food and there would be no talk of surplus land. Without subsidies and rollover tax relief the price of farmland would plummet. This would eventually reduce the cost of food since the fixed costs of farming would be significantly lowered, and farming would become much less intensive. Abolish farm subsidies, let the market decide.

The problem with so draconian an approach is that it would bankrupt most farmers and leave a landscape worked by very few people running farms of massive proportions with massive fields of low yielding crops. There would be some environmental advantages – less energy would be consumed, chemical inputs would be lower and there would be little investment in environmentally destructive practices such as drainage. But quite apart from the grievous social cost that this industrial restructuring would entail there would be major environmental disbenefits.

The market cannot deliver a large measure of that which makes Britain beautiful. The patchwork quilt of our countryside no longer makes economic sense – which is why so much of it has been unravelled. How does the immobile TV viewer lapping up the glories of the landscape, pay the market rate to the farmers who maintain it. The small farmer who has never intensified production, who is an "inefficient" producer and who will go out of business without public support, is the same farmer whose farm grows butterflies, has winding lanes, large hedges and gorse banks yellow and sweet with their smell of coconut. How can this farmer erect a turnstile to take the thin pickings that would come from charging for the joy of picnicking under the wings of skylarks?

Or should the farmer convert that uneconomic bank into a track for four-wheel-drive vehicles?

Surely we deserve better than the wastes of set-aside and the relentless pursuit of commercialisation. We can keep an attractive, farmed, countryside if we switch from subsidising each kilo of food produced to supporting management of the countryside. We would grow less per hectare; use fewer synthetic chemicals and less energy; we would have more birds and bees; and we would maintain a beautiful landscape and avoid the ghastly division of the country into weed strewn wastes and intensive wheat factories.

Let us pay farmers for the gorse and the hedges as a nation, and be proud of it!

Yours sincerely,

DAVID ASTOR.

David Astor is a farmer and businessman, and has been Chairman of the Council for the Protection of Rural England since 1983. He is a director of a number of companies, including the publisher Sinclair-Stevenson Ltd. His farm on the edge of the Cotswolds contains a 100-acre Nature Reserve.

RICHARD MABEY

Berkhamsted,
Hertfordshire.

Dear Mrs Thatcher,

Like you, I started out as a chemist, an earnest young believer in
the redemptive power of science. When I was eight I rigged up a
laboratory at the end of my father's dilapidated greenhouse, and
covered the lime-washed shelves with a collection of chemicals in
jam-jars and salad-cream bottles. I did the usual schoolboy
experiments, making gunpowder and gases, but it was the fantastic,
protean variety of matter that fascinated me most. I was amazed
that acrid gases that could cool to exquisite crystals, that the merest
whiff of current from a torch battery could split water into oxygen
and hydrogen, at all that was promised by those delicious words
allotropy and deliquescence and sublimation. At school my passion
turned into an almost unhealthy diligence, and even in the holidays
I wangled part-time jobs helping in the lab.

I think you would have approved of this mixture of studious
enthusiasm and self-help – but not the way it ended, at Oxford
(where else, you may say). It wasn't a distaste for the wrongs
committed in science's name that turned chemistry sour for me,
but something more fundamental. In those crowded laboratories in
South Parks Road I glimpsed the less appealing side of a
conventional scientific education: curiosity giving way to rote
learning, the dead hand of utility stifling the imagination, science
no longer describable as "natural philosophy". At heart I was still
that ten year old, peering in astonishment at tesselations of crystals
growing as magically and unpredictably as coral out of clear liquids.
I had no great ambition to become a sorcerer's apprentice and *direct*
them, and was happy enough being an inquisitive spectator.
Halfway through my first term I dropped science altogether,
switched to a humanities course, and took up natural history in my
spare time.

I feel sure that, as a scientist, you must once have shared that
feeling of wonder at the teeming creativity of nature. Which is why I
am so perplexed by the emphases in your political philosophy, at
your insistence that competition and struggle are more important

than cooperation and growth, and at how you reconcile your belief in choice with the new constraints imposed on children's learning experiences. It is as if you had taken your model of the world not from the cautiously optimistic and increasingly interdependent world-views of modern science, but from the darkest visions of the Victorians, in which nature – and indeed life itself – was a place of chaos and violence which could only be redeemed by human effort.

In your address to the General Assembly of the Church of Scotland in 1988, you suggested that 'abundance rather than poverty has a legitimacy which derives from the very nature of Creation'. This was widely interpreted as an economic statement, the outline of a divine mandate for wealth-creation. But I sensed a profound ecological insight behind it, though one that you seem to ignore in your political thinking. Abundance, profligacy even, is the nature of creation, the nature of Nature, if you like. But nature's abundance is not about the amassing of wealth. It is about devising ever more varied and ingenious ways of redistributing what is a fixed resource. Nature abhors monopoly as much as a vacuum, and the whole progress of evolution has been, as it were, towards *de*volution, towards invention and diversification.

Most of us were brought up to pay lip service to the principle of "the survival of the fittest" and the rule of a kind of brutish functionalism in nature. But it is now increasingly believed that what is special, *essential*, about life is its sheer exuberance. The shapes of leaves, the sheen on butterflies' wings, the detail on human faces are all ornamentation beyond any obvious usefulness. This wild, extravagant fringe to existence is the way nature works. It is part of what makes it beautiful to us, and what gives it resilience over time. Yet in the end it seems to exist for its own sake. The elaborations of a skylark's song (not the fact of it) are an irreducible mystery, an unasked, unnegotiated, solitary celebration. All nature is like this, rarely milling and struggling like a mob, but finding its spaces and seasons with grace, ingenuity and a good deal of give and take. Humans need the same freedom for aimless experiment and play if they are to grow.

There are, we would agree, dangers in using natural models for human society, and vice versa. But we are inextricably part of nature, and it may not be out of place to ask how our own social systems fit in with the ways of the larger world. I think you have already done this, and seen nature as somehow legitimising the workings of the competitive, market economy. But the ecosystem is nothing like as ruthless or as single-mindedly driven by utility and consumption as a market. It is, if anything, more like a fair, a field full of folk, some trading, some playing, some asleep and dreaming, many simply there, humming to themselves and just glad to be part of the show.

Yours sincerely,

Richard Mabey

RICHARD MABEY.

Richard Mabey is a writer, broadcaster and environmental campaigner. He writes, especially on environmental matters, for a number of publications, including the *Sunday Times*, *The Independent* and *Modern Painters*. His study of Gilbert White won the 1986 Whitbread Biography Award, and his latest book is *Home Country*, an autobiographical exploration of his 'love affair with nature'.

TED HUGHES

Dear Premier,

Treat the Environmental cataclysm as a War, on all its fronts. In other words, as an Emergency, displacing every other concern that stands in its way. Ask the people to pay for it directly. If a full public accounting is given of what is spent on what, and the attack is radical, then people will pay. Nothing would lift the morale of this country so steeply, or so unanimously. The Government's inertia on these issues has demoralised everybody, and (from my experience of what 70% of them write in their literary competitions) children are in despair.

Stop listening to scientists who have a vested interest in selling next year to keep themselves comfortable this week.

Stop despising children, i.e. double the pay of teachers. A society has only one product of any value – new generations that are trained and that know how to realise their potential. If this is true, the most important of all jobs must be that of the teachers. The teaching profession will never have the self-respect, or the personnel, to live up to this role, and to re-fashion the educational system from the inside, until their wages make it clear how the country values (a) them, (b) the training of children. No tinkering at the edges, for fear of paying some teachers too much. Just double it. Impose a tax to pay for them, and give a full public accounting to let everybody see that the money goes to the teachers – not to the Third World where it will pay gangsters to replace Tropical Forest with sterile Eucalyptus.

Read Correlli Barnett's *Audit of War*.

Yours faithfully,

Ted Hughes

TED HUGHES.

Ted Hughes is the Poet Laureate.

JOHN MAY
DAVID POWELL

Lewes, Sussex.

Dear Neil,

Absurd when you come to think about it, that Britain remains so reticent about the revolution it pioneered two centuries ago. Not so the Americans or the French. The Liberty Boys were out in strength to celebrate the bi-centenary of their Independence, while all France was *en fête* last year to commemorate the fall of the Bastille. Of course, we have always been diffident about our contribution to the Age of Revolution (damn it all, it took a Frenchman, Saint-Simon, to coin the word industrialisation), even if the men who powered it had dreams of building a world anew. Now, two centuries on, we live the consequences of their dream-turned-nightmare, but that does little to gainsay their dreams. And as they dreamt then, so we must dream now, or we will perpetuate the nightmare that you, yourself, inherited during your childhood in South Wales.

So much is easily said, of course, but much more difficult to achieve, the more so after ten years of Thatcherism. Indeed, the economic depredations of the last decade have created a dilemma for you and your colleagues which, at first glance, appears virtually insuperable, notably, how to regenerate Britain's economy to safeguard the well-being of the 56 million people of these offshore islands whilst, concurrently, safeguarding the environment on which not only their future, but the future of their children will depend.

As we see it, this is the core problem that you face, though in this you are by no means alone. To a greater or lesser extent, it is shared by governments and putative governments throughout the world: the ultimate Catch-22 that without economic growth the future of their people are imperilled, and yet unconstrained growth could well endanger the delicate eco-balance on which the survival of the globe itself depends. Even the Prime Minister appeared to have grasped the point in her Royal Society speech more than eighteen months ago. As is her way, however, the suspicion remains that fine words disguised altogether more dubious intentions.

Mrs Thatcher would be better served if she talked less, and did more to follow the lead of our EC partners who have already adopted a coherent environmental strategy – or even the example of certain American conglomerates who now accept that the business practices which applied yesterday cannot be allowed to apply tomorrow. The irony is inescapable – that in the very powerhouse of capitalism, a growing number of companies and organisations are increasingly aware that profit and environmentalism are not incompatible and that the former can be reconciled to the latter – to the benefit of both.

But if this is a lesson that Mrs Thatcher has still to learn, then equally, it is a chance for Labour to take the initiative by developing a strategy which embraces both the economic and environmental issues and in meeting the challenge, makes the change that the Party demands of itself.

Sadly, it is a missed opportunity as far as your Policy Review is concerned. Seemingly, the need to 'Compete for Prosperity' bears little, if any, relationship to the goal of creating a 'Better Quality of Life'. This is absurd, as you know better than most Neil. Indeed, the two are inextricably linked, and there is a growing constituency waiting for the Party that can balance out this equation of the future.

Our growing integration with the broader 'new Europe' presents us with an opportunity to change our perspective, to view ourselves anew in relation to a mosaic of related cultures. The new view of our planet from satellites reveals our true position in the scheme of things. The compact nature of our islands defines our character.

We look to a new government to combine the radical with the practical, the visionary with the economic, the global view with the local, the futuristic with the historic. To reintroduce the idea of citizenship, to encourage equality and denigrate elitism, to really care for the children, to truly fight for women and, above all, to keep the image of the whole earth floating in their heads.

We have all learnt a lot since, in the same week, the Rainbow Warrior was sunk and Bob Geldof staged Live Aid. Our analysis and understanding of the underlying problems has deepened. Some have become deeply cynical. Others can point to genuine progress in the last five years and a growing sense of the possible.

Three of the major social movements of the post-war period – development issues, human rights and the environment – are on a convergent path. Solutions to the world's problems will come as a result of this integration of ideas and influences. Cooperation on every level should now be the watchword of our nation.

The next decade will be defined by Chernobyl and global warming. It will see a boom in green consumerism and ethical business, a growth in Environmental Protection Agencies, the institution of precautionary principles in relation to human activities and the natural environment.

We need a true vision for a new world. The mood is abroad for real change.

Yours sincerely,

JOHN MAY
DAVID POWELL.

John May is the author of ten books, the last four of which have been written for Greenpeace. Formerly a freelance journalist for national papers and international magazines, he is now moving into film and television. David Powell is a biographer, and author of *Tom Paine: The Greatest Exile* and *Charles James Fox: Man of the People.* They are founder members of the revived Headstrong Club in Lewes.

TAM DALYELL

House of Commons,
London SW1.

Dear Mrs Thatcher,

From the time, in November 1962, when I first became your parliamentary colleague – three years after you yourself were elected – I had no doubt that your crisp approach as Parliamentary Under-Secretary of State at the Ministry of Pensions would bring you to the stratosphere of your Party. If anyone had suggested that throughout the 80s, you would have been Prime Minister, rather than Reggie Maudling or Edward Boyle, Denzil Freeth or Christopher Chataway, I would have been incredulous.

One MP, as far back as 1965, my diary tells me, did forecast that you might well become Prime Minister. It was your "pair" Charlie Pannell, the no-nonsense AUEW Member for West Leeds, Minister of Public Buildings and Works, for whom I worked when Terry Boston, his PPS, was in Australia. It was through arranging "pairs" that I first knew you, and your decisive nature. Charlie, who admired you, thought you were a 'toughie'. Dick Crossman, for whom I worked as PPS, thought you were 'a lady to be reckoned with' and that you would soon become the First Lady and Barbara Castle of the Tory Party. Though he opined that the qualities that make a good Prime Minister are more likely to be found in a woman than in a man, he did not conceive circumstances in which the Tory Party would choose a woman. I myself shared their good opinion of you, and this was re-inforced when as Secretary of State for Education you saved the Open University, which many Conservatives regarded as a Harold Wilson "gimmick".

My subsequent well-chronicled anger with you, as Prime Minister – which is very different from the normal come-and-go of adversarial politics – relates basically to two unpardonable habits of yours.

First, you use difficult situations, such as the South Atlantic, or the position in the coalfields, for your own personal political advantage, rather than trying to resolve problems. Your use of David Hart to ferment problems among the miners was plain wicked. And, as Sara Keays's book corroborates, in recording Cecil

Parkinson's reactions on 18 April 1982, my impression formed during our last personal conversation on 21 April, 1982, in your room in the Commons, that you wanted a fight, and military victory in the Falklands, rather than a long-term solution to an Anglo-Argentine dispute, was right. The House of Commons assumed that with your Foreign Secretary, Francis Pym, in Washington, you were doing all possible to get peace, when, in fact, a short war suited your domestic political purposes.

My second basic complaint is that when you are in a tight political corner, as over the Law Officer's Letter disclosure and Westland, or over the loss of Nigel Lawson, as your Chancellor of the Exchequer, you resort to being 'economical with the truth' (to use your Cabinet Secretary's expression).

Let us now concentrate on a subject about which I am deeply alarmed, and where, by your decision to ear-mark £100 million, you have shown goodwill and imagination, the rain-forests.

Already knowing the West African and Borneo rain-forest, I went in 1989 to the Xingu River, in the Amazonian water system. If the burning, clearance and destruction of the eco-system continues on its current scale in Eastern Brazil, by the processes of evapo-transpiration which, as a scientist, you understand better than most MPs, the rains which hopscotch across the Amazon will be cut off at source.

The dry periods will be larger. Forest fires will rage, as never before. Desperate cattle-men will clear more ground to feed their miserable animals. Deprived of rain, many species will simply wither away, and perish. There will be a botanical and biological holocaust. Millions of species, as yet unexamined for their medicinal properties, will have perished. Nor, is it simply a matter of believing, as I do, in that a world deprived of many species of Amazonian parrot is a poorer world.

Were the Amazon destroyed, the air currents would probably change. The westerly currents which strike the high Andes, and return across South America to parallel the Gulf Stream, and give us our warm, prevailing south-west winds would not happen. London would have the climate of Labrador, and Edinburgh the climate of Northern Labrador.

On the time scale, we cannot be sure. But, we do know that in the last decade, economic pandemonium was caused by El Niño switching her habits. And, the poor old mammoth was not a tundra-eating animal. It was, (from the contents of its stomach), a feeder on temperate or semi-tropical plants. The mammoth was caught by a climatic flip.

What can be done? You are right to have used your position as Prime Minister to help focus attention on Global Climate Change. Even if it wastes money, you should follow the advice of the working parties you have set up.

But, on rain-forests, the problem is more difficult. Countries with forests do not want their sovereignty insulted. For pity's sake, don't throw your proverbial handbag at them, lecturing them on what they ought to do. Much of the trouble has poverty as its cause, and this is inextricably bound up with burgeoning Third World debt.

This, in time, will only be alleviated by painstaking discussion with governments and banks throughout the world, so that no one rich country is disadvantaged in relation to its rich competitors, and no one bank, such as the Midland or Lloyds, who have lent heavily to South America, being disadvantaged in relation to other banks.

Margaret, if I may use the friendly form of address I used in the first twenty years, 1962-1982, we knew each other, you could use your talents as a knocker-together of leaders and your undoubted international reputation, to perform an historic service – steps to protect the world's rain-forests.

Yours sincerely,

Tam Dalyell

TAM DALYELL, MP.

Tam Dalyell has been MP (Labour) for West Lothian and Linlithgow since 1962. He has been a prominent backbench campaigner on issues including the Falklands War, the Westland affair, the bombing of Libya, and the destruction of the rain-forests, and he has written a weekly column for *New Scientist* since 1967. His books include *Portrait of Dick Crossman* (1989), *Misrule: How Mrs Thatcher Deceived Parliament* (1987), *One Man's Falklands* (1983), and *Ship School: Dunera* (1962).

ANN CLWYD

*House of Commons,
London SW1.*

Dear Mrs Thatcher,

There are a thousand million people living in poverty overseas. In ten years in power you have done nothing to help them.

Your Government has presided over historic cuts in overseas aid. What little aid Britain has given has done more to help British exports than to assist the struggling poor, malnourished children, and over-worked women. This Government has been happy to leave developing countries to deal with their massive and mounting debt burden, multiplying environmental problems, and sinking commodity prices for their exports, on their own.

When Labour left office, our overseas aid accounted for 0.51% of our Gross National Product (GNP), and we were working towards the United Nations aid target of 0.7%. Since then, it has slumped to an historic low of just 0.32% of GNP. From being one of the most generous donors in Europe, we have become one of the most miserly, ranking 14th out of the 18 members of the Organisation for Economic Cooperation and Development.

You said in the 1983 General Election Campaign that 'when economic circumstances permit we will move towards the UN target of 0.7% of GNP'. Last year you said 'we now have a higher standard of living than we have ever known'. Clearly the problem is not that we cannot afford as much Third World aid as our European partners give, but that the Government just doesn't care.

If you had maintained the Labour Government's aid commitment, the Third World would be better off by £6.4 billion. Just one tenth of that would pay for the eradication of six infectious diseases – polio, tetanus, measles, diphtheria, whooping cough and tuberculosis. These diseases kill 20 children a year in Britain, but in the Third World they claim three million lives every year. Where poverty is so extreme, a bit of aid can go a long way: a life-saving salt and sugar rehydration solution, for children with diarrhoea, costs just 7 pence. Yet every year, four million children die from diarrhoea.

But of course, a bigger aid programme probably would not be

spent on saving these children's lives, because in the last ten years, the aid programme has focussed less and less on poverty alleviation. Aid has become more commercialised: more than two thirds of the aid budget is spent inside the UK. Boosting British exports is fine, but it is gross injustice to use money supposedly intended for Third World development.

Aid has been diverted away from local development projects to supporting economic adjustment programmes of the World Bank and IMF. The poor have taken the brunt of the severe economic reforms demanded by these two institutions. They have suffered declining living standards, disappearing jobs and slashed government services. Other donors have stepped in to help protect the poor from the worst effects, while encouraging policy-makers to pay special attention to their needs. But not the British Government. Your Government just piggy-backed onto the IMF's demands, repeating the old rhetoric about economic discipline with no regard for who pays the price; oblivious of the need to maintain health and education services today if tomorrow's workforce is ever to take advantage of a leaner, more stable economy.

If you were go "walkabout" through the villages and shanty-towns of the Third World, you would soon see what is needed. You would see women spending hours each day collecting water for their families. Massive hydro-electric dams don't help them but a local bore-well would. In the back rooms, you would see a woman dying in childbirth. Cuts in government health spending won't help her, but maternal health programmes could save her and the half a million women like her every year. You would see babies dying from powdered baby food, bought with their families' meagre savings, then mixed with dirty river water. Free market ideologies will do nothing for them: strict rules on health and safety information for international companies could prevent one million baby-milk deaths each year.

In the cities you would see sprawling slums, a mass of cardboard and humanity, and smell the stench of open sewage. Aid-subsidised British exports will not help them but an open market here for the goods they manufacture and process would boost their incomes. You probably would not see the courageous men and women struggling against repressive government and military might. Back-patting official visits will not bring them to light, but support for their organisations, harsh words and sanctions for their governments, and international action will.

In Africa, you would see women walking further afield each day to collect firewood for cooking. National forestry plans for loggers will not help them but support for local tree planting, provision of seeds, education in forestry, and assistance in more efficient cooking methods would save time, energy, and trees. In Latin America, you would see indigenous people losing the forest – their home, their source of food, clothes and medicine, and way of life – to loggers, miners, and ranchers. The Tropical Forestry Action Plan, that you so keenly support, will help logging companies but it won't help the indigenous tribes, now disappearing at the rate of one a year.

In Cambodia, you would see the few doctors treating victims of Khmer Rouge land mines, with no medicines, not even pain killers. In Vietnam, you would see basic facilities, such as water pipes and sewage systems collapsing for lack of funds. Continuing the game of super-power politics will not help these countries. Only an end to their international isolation and an inflow of foreign funds will get them back on their feet.

Despite some progress on some fronts, the problems of the Third World are mounting not diminishing. The eighties were indeed a lost decade: as Third World debt doubled to $1.3 trillion, development ground to a halt. In the poorest countries, health spending per head fell by one half. In Latin America and the Caribbean, income per person shrank by 7%.

The new challenge of the 90s is to achieve development without destroying the environment. Your green rhetoric has barely concealed the Government's inaction. A total reassessment of priorities is needed instead to target aid on conservation, clean technology, renewable energy, environmental research, and building the capacity of citizens and governments to invest in environmental care. The UK should not support multilateral institutions that recommend deflation and export promotion, with no regard for environmental effects.

The cost of clean development will be more than developing countries can afford and major new international funds will be needed. It is estimated that the cost to developing countries of complying with the Montreal Protocol on chlorofluorocarbons will be between $3 and $6 billion, and the cost of energy efficiency and renewable energy will be around $85 billion. The entire world will suffer if these investments are not made. Instead of holding back international agreements, Britain should be spurring the international community into action.

I have little hope that your Government will, at this late stage, come to realise the vast needs and opportunities in the Third World. I can only assure you that the next Labour Government will make Third World development a priority and we shall all benefit when developing economies prosper, the appalling waste of lives and talents due to poverty is stopped, and comprehensive policies are implemented to protect the vast environmental resources in the Third World.

Yours sincerely,

ANN CLWYD, MP
Shadow Minister for
Overseas Development and Cooperation.

Ann Clwyd is MP (Labour) for Cynon Valley, and Shadow Secretary of State for Overseas Development. Elected to the Shadow Cabinet in 1989, she was previously Deputy Spokeswoman on Women's Affairs and Education. She is the only woman MP in Wales, elected in a 1984 by-election, and previously represented Mid and West Wales in the European Parliament (1979-84). She is a former member of the Socialist Group Executive and of the National Executive Committee of the Labour Party.

PETER HAIN

London SW15.

Dear Mrs Thatcher,

You have always prided yourself on standing up for Britain. But is your policy of relaxing pressure on the South African Government really in our interests as a country?

Let's leave aside the fact that Nelson Mandela, the ANC and the overwhelming tide of black South African opinion favours sanctions and increased pressure on the Government until it moves to abolish apartheid. Having ignored them in the past, there is no reason to suppose you will be persuaded by their appeals now.

Let's leave aside the fact that you have been willing to apply sanctions against the Soviet bloc when Stalinism reigned. The boycott of the 1980 Moscow Olympics and sanctions against Poland in the early 1980s spring to mind. So opposition to sanctions is presumably not one of principle for you.

Let's also leave aside the record of pressure on apartheid. You will doubtless know of the countless occasions when sanctions have produced immediate and tangible concessions from Pretoria.

Sport is a notable example. The progressive imposition of a worldwide sports boycott from 1970 onwards produced a momentum for change previously unthinkable. As I recall, you were originally opposed to the sports boycott campaigns at the time, but along with others inside and outside South Africa subsequently conceded its merit and its proven record of success.

The fundamental – some might say elementary – point is that white South Africa has *only* ever changed when forced to do so. This was certainly true over sport, but perhaps the key example is the Government's sudden switch under President de Klerk which followed pressure from white business.

As you will be aware, since the mid 1980s, the South African economy has been starved of international investment and loan finance. Talk to any white family (as I did when I made a secret visit to South Africa in December 1989) and you will find an anxiety about living standards unheard of from a group which for decades has enjoyed a lifestyle of affluence. Talk to business analysts and company executives and you will find a serious lack of confidence in the future. The 1980s international sanctions – for the investment and financial restrictions have been sanctions in all but name – have indeed been effective.

I doubt whether you really understand the white South Africa psyche. You talk of giving carrots and encouragement. But all the time they are laughing behind your back. They see you as one of "us": someone who parrots their wishes and speaks for them in the world. And while you continue to do so, they will feel under no requirement to change.

The curious thing is that you clearly understood this with your bold initiative to resolve the Rhodesian crisis in 1979. You pulled the rug from underneath Ian Smith's rebellious whites. And they acquiesced in the eclipse of white minority rule with remarkable equanimity precisely because you ensured that *they had no alternative.* They knew their time was up.

Why not apply the same logic to South Africa? The ideology of white rule, the fears and the prejudices, are much the same in Pretoria in the 1990s as they were in Salisbury during the 1970s.

Otherwise there is a real danger of the historic opportunity which has emerged in South Africa recently disappearing as negotiations are bogged down in white intransigence and as tension rises on both sides.

For the point is that sanctions and pressure are the best protection against a *violent* transition. They offer an alternative strategy which is also the best hope for a *democratic* future. History shows that a violent transition provides infertile ground for democracy to be nurtured.

But even if these arguments, too, are best left aside because you will not be persuaded by the evidence, how is Britain's interest best protected in the unfolding drama of Southern Africa? What policy will best safeguard UK foreign investments (still overwhelmingly the dominant foreign stake in the country)?

The only realistic future for South Africa is one of majority rule. Already blacks have been flexing their economic power as consumers, by boycotting white companies to achieve a political objective. And they have been very successful in so doing.

But when they run the country, are they going to do any favours for a Britain which has shunned them in the past, which has defied their political appeals? A Britain which under your Premiership has, *alone* in the world, stood alongside the white minority rulers in opposing sanctions? Or are they going to look to those countries which supported them during the long, bitter and bleak years of repression and mass poverty?

Don't you accept that the European countries which have respected the EC's support for sanctions, and the white Commonwealth countries – Australia, New Zealand and Canada – which have supported the Commonwealth's policy where you have roundly flouted it, and the USA which has also deserted you – don't you accept that these countries who include our strongest competitors are going to get more favourable treatment and trade terms than Britain?

And what about the rest of Africa? It deeply resents your stance of prim isolation in steadfastly remaining Pretoria's friend. As a reborn South Africa looks North and uses its economic power to spur Africa into a new era of growth and development, Britain will be left in the cold. Yet the African market is huge. Our historic ties potentially equip us to make the running in economic trade and development.

The tragedy is that our policy towards South Africa is not only against the interests of the black majority, it is also against the interests of the British people.

Yours sincerely,

PETER HAIN.

Peter Hain is an anti-apartheid campaigner and Labour parliamentary candidate. He has written 11 books on politics and socialism, and is Head of Research for the Union of Communication Workers.

JAN MORRIS

Llanystumdwy,
Gwynedd, Cymru.

Annwyl Mr Kinnock,

There is only one issue specific to Wales: the survival of the Welsh nation, by which I mean a nation speaking its own language and honouring its own culture, history and traditions.

Politically it doubtless seems to you unimportant. Only a fifth of the Welsh speak Welsh nowadays (Mrs Kinnock among them of course), and the earthier matters of social welfare and economic well-being, which are really common to all the countries of the United Kingdom, are the ones that win or lose votes. Your party as a whole, I am sure, regards Wales as just another region, like the North West or the South East, with a tiresome scattering of nationalist zealots best disregarded.

I am such a zealot, and I would like to place before you an historical judgement that may well be passed upon you if you ever become Prime Minister: that during your term of office you presided over the death of Wales. I do not mean of course the disappearance of the "region", to which you may well give extra prominence. I mean the death of that small nation which has for a thousand years defied the proximity of England to retain its own identity, its own pride and above all its own language, Cymraeg, one of the oldest literary languages in Europe, which was producing great poets six centuries before Chaucer was born.

The reason is that the unrestricted pressure of market forces, unleashed so recklessly by Mrs Thatcher, is proving too much for a fragile balance maintained, with extreme difficulty, for a thousand years – the awkward equilibrium which has enabled Welshness to survive in the shadow of so mighty and so alien a neighbour. By the diligence and sacrifice of Welsh patriots in many generations, by the intermittent shrewdness of governments in Westminster, large parts of Wales have remained thoroughly Welsh in language and in style. Recently there have even been signs that Cymraeg is past the worst of its decline, and that the English-speaking Welsh, too, are regaining their attachment to their oldest roots and traditions. Until a year or two ago I myself thought that ours was a struggle which, while it probably could never be won, would never be lost either.

Now all is changing. An apparently irresistible flood of English settlers is, before our very eyes, obliterating the old Wales. They are not mere second-homers, but immigrants, moving into those parts of the country that have remained most Welsh – the beautiful and once remote districts of the north-west which have always been the ultimate strongholds of Welshness. They are buying houses at prices no young Welsh people can afford, they are taking over those post offices, corner shops, pubs and cafés that have traditionally been the exchanges of the Welsh tradition. Hideously backed by the greedy power of tourism, which the Thatcher Government has blindly encouraged, they are occupying large slabs of the country as tragically as any invading army. They generally care nothing for the language and the culture, often supposing themselves indeed still to be in England, and their English-speaking children, like grey squirrels driving out red, are fast dominating the country schools which have been the nurseries of Welshness.

You may perhaps argue (though I am not so sure – you are a Welshman after all) that the end of Wales would not matter, would indeed be no more than a political relief. Or you might reason that Wales would survive anyway, with or without its language and its ancient heritage – is there anyone more Welsh, you may well say, than one of your English-speaking, rugby-playing, choir-singing, hard-drinking, Labour-voting stalwarts of the South Wales valleys?

But there is a profounder issue here, almost an abstract issue. Just as a Welshman cannot really be a complete Welshman if he does not speak Welsh, any more than an Englishman could be complete without a knowledge of English, so Wales without the Welsh language, and without the brotherhood, the values and all the allusions that go with it, would no longer be a nation. It *would* be just another region. The continued flooding of Wales with English people, money and values may well mean the end of history for the Welsh, which is perhaps why the Tories so encourage it – as you know, the only two motorways in Wales are both roads built to facilitate movement out of England.

If you allow it to happen you will be presiding over a consummation of infinite sadness – the end of something old, beloved and truly beautiful. On the other hand if you can stop the rot you will not only be remembered in your own country as one of its great patriots, but may also be ahead of the political game: for is it not likely that the emergence of a federal Europe will give altogether new consequence to the minority nations, the nations which are not States – the Basques, the Corsicans, the Catalans, the Bretons, the Scots and the Welsh?

Welsh Wales can be saved, Mr Kinnock – it is almost too late, but not quite. We need a Welsh Assembly first, of course, to give us some introductory measure of control over our own destinies. We need legislation, unhampered by ridiculous interpretations of the Race Relations Act, to control the ruinous influx of strangers – if Jersey can do it, why shouldn't we? We need a new and modern attitude towards what is now more and more regarded, all over the world, as the blight of mass tourism. We need a truly whole-hearted and financially generous campaign of support for the Welsh language, presided over perhaps (and I speak as a fervent republican) by the titular Prince of Wales.

We need, in short, a few gestures of magnificence – quixotic gestures if you like – in support of a cause that is not logical to over-logical minds, not statistically significant to second-rate statisticians, but noble in itself: the survival of an idea, a language, a loyalty and a love. Is there any other British cause, in or out of the pages of this book, which can be pleaded with such romantic passion?

Dymuniadau gorau,

JAN MORRIS.

Jan Morris is the author of *The Matter of Wales*. She has also written books about the British Empire, Venice, Oxford, Hong Kong, Spain and Manhattan, the novel *Last Letters from Hav* (shortlisted for the Booker Prize), and two memoirs, *Conundrum* and *Pleasures of a Tangled Life*, together with six collected volumes of travel essays.

ANNE SMITH

Glasgow.

Dear Mrs Thatcher,

Just a wee note from Scotland (remember Scotland? North of Watford? No? You spoke to the General Assembly of the Church here a year or two ago – men with their collars reversed, women in hats: economic morality? The place you dump the nuclear waste? That's right, Malcolm's fief: *that* Scotland).

As I was saying, just a wee note to encourage you to keep up the good work, and while we of course shall go on not voting for you, we shall not cease to appreciate the logic of your policies. It was no coincidence that Adam Smith, who gave his name to the Institute which I hear advises you on the most direct routes to your economic miracle, was born here.

It makes sense to have tested out the Poll Tax in a country which voted so overwhelmingly for the other party. You had nothing to lose in Scotland – and you're no' daft, you stopped yourself from losing the little you have just in the nick by extending the rebates to us. That was generous. I'm sure even all the non-payers felt the warmth of that gesture, huddled round their unlicensed TVs, eagerly charting the progress of the economic miracle, night after night, till the power's cut off.

Oh aye, we're following your progress, never you worry! Privatise the lot: why not? Selling the family silver, auld Macmillan opined. With a name like his he should have known better – who needs silver forks as long as they've got fingers? And just look at the social benefits! British Telecom, for example...don't think it's passed us by how these chat-lines provide a channel for masses of filth that before privatisation had nowhere to go. Never mind that the sewage under the cities is getting to be in the same situation – you by a stroke of genius provided a mental sewage system that pays its own way. Maybe you could make a thing of it in your next campaign? (Mr Gummer would be the boy to put that one across.)

Speaking of the mind and social benefits – no, no, I'm not going to criticise you for turning the bereft out of the mental institutions and onto the streets – between them and the lager louts, city life is regaining the colourful unpredictability it used to have at the turn of the century (the nineteenth century, that is, but what's wrong with a bit of nostalgia, say I). Speaking, as I said, of the mind and social benefits – we up here are fascinated with what you've been doing re. higher education.

I mean, take rating university departments according to the amount of sponsorship they attract: man, you pu'd a rare stroke there! For if there was one thing the matter with universities, it was that they were far too full of yon intellectuals living off the fat of the land and producing nothing but hot air. This cute wee idea of starving out the arts faculties and the law, now, is pure dead brilliant. In one move you'll have deprived the opposition of its main source of recruitment and kept the oiks out of the opera. Nae borra, eh?

The cutbacks in the libraries too – these are particularly effective in schools in the poor areas here. Literacy is power, and look what happened when the peasants got power in Eastern Europe. Seventy years of sheer misery till you managed to show Mr Gorbachev the error of their ways. Oh aye, when we live once more in a pastoral idyll like at the time of the Clearances, we'll know whose memory to tug our forelocks to!

Mind you, it puts the Scots in a dilemma, us having always been all for education, and you'll probably find that we're as little contented with intellectual as with physical poverty. But there again, since when did philosophy put caviare on the blinis, sez you? What did the law do for the directors of Guinness or the Fayed brothers? And all that money that would have been spent on making socialist philistines out of potentially contented peasants can go on the defence of the country, where it's sorely needed.

You'll have to watch, though, that some ex-comprehensive over-educated (at our expense) do-gooder doesn't start snooping around the perks of the armed forces and pointing out that, for example, a lass of 21 with one A-level can make £12,000 p.a. doing nothing but arranging the flowers for regimental dinners in between the odd recruitment drive, while her sister the nurse with years of training takes home £4 or £5K less. Privatise the Health Service as fast as you can, is the answer to that one.

Incidentally, I hope you'll keep up the good work of reducing the industrial base of the economy. That should get the green vote. It's already doing wonders for the ecosphere. I was through in Fife last week and noticed that the nerve-wracking whirr of the colliery winding-machinery was silent at last, thanks to you (well, not entirely: Mr Wilson played his part there, it has to be said). Pay no heed to the mutterings and moanings of the whey-faced dole-scroungers with their so-called community values. We Scots are used to poverty and will find a way in time. We are natural philosophers who realise that if you're not worrying about how to spin out your giro to pay the Poll Tax, you're worrying about how to spin out your salary to cover the increased mortgage rate. Everything's relative; nothing changes much, only superficially, and we toddle on as we ay did.

Speaking of which, again: should the worst happen and Mr Kinnock's party win the election, don't waste your well-earned retirement fretting about Scotland. His policies are not that much different from your own and anyway, the Labour Party has always been able to ignore us, because they know we'll vote for them – that's the price we pay for our wrongheaded old Scottish ideals of democracy, brotherhood etc. as promulgated by the dangerously radical poet Burns. We live in the past and the rent is outrageous.

Got to go – the yuppification of Glasgow proceeds apace and I'd hate to miss a minute of it. And I've an appointment to visit a school that was half burned down last year (it's still half burned down this year) (You might mention it to Malcolm? No? Oh well) –

Cheerio the noo!

Anne Smith

ANNE SMITH.

Dr Anne Smith is a journalist and Chief Executive of Book Trust (Scotland). Her last book was *Women Remember: Interviews with women in their eighties* (Routledge, 1989). She was the founder-editor of the *Literary Review*.

IAN PAISLEY

Belfast,
Northern Ireland.

Dear Mrs Thatcher,

It is with a deep sense of disillusionment I pen this letter.

When you first donned the mantle of leadership of this United Kingdom of Great Britain and Northern Ireland, you presented yourself as a Prime Minister dedicated to return our people to a reclaiming of those great principles and code of conduct which gained for us the well deserved and universally acknowledged prefix 'Great' before our national identification 'Britain'.

Your singlemindedness which was most refreshing in our political life acted as a cleansing salt in the stagnant pool of the body politic. It heralded the dawning of what at first seemed a new day for us all.

But alas how quickly the Thatcher silver became dross and the Maggie wine became mixed with water as far as Northern Ireland was concerned. You judged not the fatherless, and the case of the widows of Ulster brought no appropriate response from your heart. You forsook your singlemindedness and a doublemindedness took over, resulting in the appalling fact that you who were once the most respected and most popular Prime Minister are now the most rejected in modern history.

Surely that should cause even you great searching of heart.

This drastic and tragic change, I believe, stems from that darkest of all days in Ulster's recent history when you repudiated every semblance of democratic principle and in an act of treachery sold the Ulster people like cattle on the hoof into the hands of their traditional enemies in Dublin.

That act of treachery was vile enough in itself but the hypocrisy of your comment at the time would do credit to Beelzebub himself. As you poised to sign the diktat you stated that the young men and women of the security forces who had been murdered by the IRA had compelled you to enter into the so-called Anglo-Irish Agreement. In other words you stated that you owed them this act of treachery.

To think that you, madam, who pose as the great law and order, anti-terrorist stateswoman of the world, the defender of the democratic faith, the scourge of dictatorship, the Iron Lady who will not bend before threats and assaults, would help forward the IRA's goal and hand part control of Her Majesty's territory in Ireland to that well-known terrorist sanctuary provider – the Irish Republic.

What right have you to claim the authority of the ballot box and cheer on the downtrodden majorities of Eastern Europe in their righteous struggle for majority rule when in your own back yard you have entered into arrangements to deny to the Ulster people their inalienable right to be ruled as free men and women?

What right have you to promise any future Republican majority their goal to break up the United Kingdom and thrust Northern Ireland out from under the Crown while at the same time refusing to grant to the present Unionist majority the right to be governed as any other part of the United Kingdom?

What right have you to institutionalise the religious faith of the Ulster people so that you can hound Protestants out of their jobs and by the most jesuitical and sectarian law which has ever been devised since the dark ages of the Romish Inquisition seek to push them into a Roman Catholic State which denies the most simple and basic human rights to its citizens?

What right have you to deny the right to fly the flag of this United Kingdom in this part of Her Majesty's dominion and at the same time provide police protection for the flag of Haughey's republic?

What right have you to close down by force the Northern Ireland Assembly, which your own Government set up, just because its members refused to bow the knee to your dictatorship?

What right have you to shackle the security forces from defeating the murdering scum of IRA terrorism and allowing Ulster to deteriorate into another Lebanon?

What right have you never once to praise the law-abiding Protestant majority population of Ulster from whom you get the vast majority of your security recruits who by your policy are savagely murdered by the IRA?

What right have you to refuse to come to grips with Mr Haughey on extradition and his savage attacks on the gallant Ulster Defence Regiment?

What right have you to allow members of that Regiment and also members of the Royal Ulster Constabulary to become scapegoats to appease the SDLP and all their fellow travellers?

As a British Prime Minister you have betrayed British rights.

As a Unionist Prime Minister in Ulster you have destroyed the Union of Northern Ireland and Great Britain.

As a Democratic Prime Minister you have sold out democracy in this part of the United Kingdom.

I am but the advocate of the majority population, elected to that position by the largest number of votes ever cast for a UK politician, but you stand indicted by the thousands of Ulster's honoured dead, by the thousands of bereaved ones ever over-shadowed with their tremendous griefs and by the vast majority of decent folks whom you have given as a prey to bloodthirsty Irish Republicanism.

You may disregard their indictment now and shrug off these charges with disdain but 'the damned spot' is unremovable. It has already blotted your history, tarnished your rule and will eventually, if you repent not, lead to your fall.

I leave you to ponder the word of God from the lips of the Old Testament prophet.

'Then she that is mine enemy shall see it, and shame shall cover her which said unto me, Where is the Lord thy God? mine eyes shall behold her; now shall she be trodden down as the mire of the streets.' Micah 7:10.

Yours sincerely,

Ian R. K. Paisley

IAN PAISLEY, MP, MEP. *Eph 6:19+20*

Dr Ian Paisley is MP for North Antrim and MEP for Northern Ireland. He is Leader of the Ulster Democratic Unionist Party and Moderator of the Free Presbyterian Church of Ulster. He has held a Westminster seat for over 20 years and has been a Member of the European Parliament for over ten years. In one European Parliament election he polled 230,351 votes, the highest number ever by a British politician.

FINTAN O'TOOLE

Dublin,
Ireland.

Dear Margaret,

Now that you've nothing left to lose, now that the game is up, you have the kind of freedom you've probably never known before. Your going may be inevitable, but the manner of your going is a matter of choice. And since the messianic glint that was always in your eye has turned into a bonfire, you'll be thinking about history and your place in it. If you're honest, you'll be thinking that all you've really done is to ride out the death spasms of an old post-war world and to kill it off in the meanest of ways. You have been the undertaker of a certain period in history, not a midwife. Even your finest hour, the Falklands "victory" will be no more than a cranky, perverse footnote to the death of Empire. And if you allow yourself to entertain any of these thoughts (they certainly won't entertain you), you might also remember that there is a real, living history that you can still leave your mark on, that there is something you might be remembered for that isn't mean.

I'm talking, of course, about the question of Northern Ireland, a piece of history that is bedevilled by being both yours and ours, a question that you have come for many of us here, to embody. 'More substance in our enmities than in our love' one of our poets once wrote, and the extent to which you are hated has made you a substantial figure in Ireland. Some people, the more stupid ones, hate you simply because you are a British Prime Minister and therefore nothing you might ever do could be right. Others hate you because, after all, Britain is, for many of us, a kind of home and your domestic policies hurt Irish people too. But there are others still who hate you because they recognise in you a mirror-image of themselves, see your nationalistic arrogance, your blinkered visions, as the unacceptable face of their own. For all of them, and for all the others who just want the blood to stop flowing, you occupy an extraordinary position in the Irish psyche, a position where you are as much a symbol as a real presence, where your manner of speaking is even more important than what you say.

By now, you will be getting impatient. You will be saying that on this issue you have changed more than on any other. And it is true that you have gone from a black-and-white view of the question (with the Protestants as the Falkland Islanders and the IRA as the Argies) to a grey-and-grey one, boredom tempered by outbursts of impatience. You have sent reasonably intelligent men to run the place, and you have listened more to what they tell you. And all this psychic stuff will strike you as the worst sort of nonsense. That, in a sense is precisely the problem.

The problem is all about ambivalence, and ambivalence is not something that has much place in your view of the world. It is the ambivalence of a place that refuses to be one thing or the other – British or Irish – and insists on being both. And it is also more specifically the ambivalence of people of my background, Irish, Catholic and nationalist, about how they should regard people on the same island but of a different background: British, Protestant and, in its own way, nationalist. This is where you come in. Many, many people from an Irish Catholic background desperately need to free themselves from the power of a simple myth of Irish freedom and British oppression. They need to do so for their own sakes, so that they can see the world they inhabit more clearly, and for the sake of the Protestants, so that they can feel the sense of a siege being lifted and start to think freely about their relationship to the rest of the world. And this means freeing themselves of you and everything you represent as a symbol of that peculiar mixture of arrogance and bafflement which tends to characterise British attitudes to Ireland. You can help them to do this without in any way conceding to the savagery of the self-appointed saviours of the people.

It is a question of imagination and therefore, I suppose, a difficult question for you. It is about having the imagination to feel what the things you do might mean to people of a different culture, with a different sense of history. It is about understanding that every shot to kill, every casual insult at a roadblock, every rubber bullet that is okay for Belfast but not okay for a riot in London, every time you say that the UDR is a fine body of men without nodding in the direction of the murders that have been committed by members and former members, every time you ignore the pleas to release Irish prisoners in Britain – specifically the Birmingham Six, whom you must know are innocent – every time you curl your lip and start hectoring Ireland, you play the role that the IRA and their supporters so desperately need you to play. Every Gibraltar is a rock for them to hurl, not at you, but at the Protestants. Every lecture you give stirs up an equal and opposite retreat into useless, sterile, self-pitying but nonetheless powerful emotions.

The hatred, though, is also an opportunity. Coming from you, signs of graciousness and imagination would mean much more than similar signs from those who will come after you. They can change policies; you, because you have become a symbol, can also change minds and hearts. If you were to ask for the Birmingham Six to be freed, if you were to say that never again will the rule of law be defended by a breach of the spirit of the law, if you were to say that your only interest was i.i creating structures to embody mutual respect, it would be immensely significant. You could banish a spectre, lay the ghost of a certain kind of England as seen from Ireland. You could become an exorcist rather than an undertaker.

Yours sincerely,

FINTAN O'TOOLE.

Fintan O'Toole is a columnist and critic with the *Irish Times*. Born in Dublin in 1958, he has been arts editor of the *Sunday Tribune* and editor of *Magill*. His books include *The Politics of Magic* (1987), a study of the Irish playwright Thomas Murphy, and *No More Heroes: A Radical Guide to Shakespeare* (1990), both published by Raven Arts Press.

BRUCE KENT

London N4.

Dear Neil,

I don't envy you the way you now have to live. Yours is a world of minders and managers. Public opinion polls have become your yardsticks. People like me are dangerous and to be avoided. The pressures on you must be dreadful. Whom can you trust? One major slip and the media pundits can turn you into yesterday's man overnight.

So why am I writing? Partly to assure you that I and others have not forgotten the Neil Kinnock of yesterday. I think you have been pushed into your present lack of radical conviction by minders who have told you at all costs to placate our right-wing media. How otherwise, when David Frost asked you about socialism, was it that you did not come back in ringing terms about justice, sharing, and a community of people national and international where the price tag is not the measure of everything?

There is actually no way of placating our media. Throw them one bone and they will only want two. All you can do is speak over the top of them with passion. I want to hear again the younger Kinnock speaking from the heart. You know perfectly well that you aren't going down in history as a Disraeli or a Gladstone. You could be valued by future generations for honesty and conscience.

Tell the people that as democracy comes to the East we could do with some more of it here at home. A second chamber on a hereditary basis is not just antiquated: it's offensive. Say so with passion. An electoral system that can give one party an overwhelming victory on a minority of votes has to be unjust. Say so with conviction. How exactly we reform that system is quite another matter. That women should be so grossly underrepresented in the House of Commons is absurd. No more resolutions or rhetoric on this please. Just make it clear that in your view all safe Labour seats should be fought by women candidates until justice is seen to be done in your party.

And while you are at it let's have some plain speaking on MPs. They do not need more money. They do need decent working conditions and sensible hours of work. Call for the scrapping of all consultancies, union handouts, second jobs and other forms of feather bedding. Let's hear something radical from you about our old-boy judicial system, our self-policing police forces and our disgusting prisons. It was left to Chris Mullin to lead the way on justice for the Guildford Four and the Birmingham Six. Why play the media game when it comes to party discipline? James Callaghan, Peter Shore and John Gilbert – just to name a few of your right-wingers – openly repudiated Labour's defence policy through two elections and did the party great harm. But no censure for them. Frank Field gets deselected and then threatens to stand against our official party candidate. Yet he gets the Party blessing and consolation. Why? If you are trying to placate Joe Haines or Peter Jenkins forget it. Your voice has to be heard over theirs – and has to have your heart in it.

Worldwide, new opportunities are opening up everywhere. E. P. Thompson's great Appeal of 1980 called for a united, democratic demilitarised Europe. Now it is happening at a pace no one could have expected. Let's hear from you now about a wider world. About the United Nations, the World Court and the Helsinki process. Give us your vision of a Europe that is something more than an economic partnership between the rich West and the poor East.

The defence policy review forced on you by the Kaufmans and the Mandelsons at the 1989 conference is already in tatters. It was a shameful patchwork of contradictions at its best. History has now given you a new opportunity – economies all round the world are having to plan for a shift from swords to ploughshares. The Labour Party, with the unions, should be at the front of this process – not rubbishing its own overwhelming democratic opinion.

A little personal conviction about nuclear "defence" would be very timely too. Trident is not just expensive – it's stupid. There is no conceivable threat to Britain to which an intelligent response would be to risk blowing up the world. In fact today people realise in their guts that the real threats facing humanity are collective ones ranging from pollution to exploding populations.

There is much more that might be said to encourage as well as to criticise. Your real friends are confused and hurt by what has happened to you and our party in the last few years. You may feel that your activists have not sufficiently understood your problems. But don't forget – I want you to win the next election because I want with you to turn our country towards social justice. A Kinnock standing for anything else would not be worth fighting for and would not be the Kinnock I remember.

Good wishes,

Yours sincerely,

Bruce Kent.

BRUCE KENT.

Bruce Kent is Chair of CND and President of the International Peace Bureau. Born in 1929, he read Law at Oxford, and was an active Catholic priest for 30 years. A supporter of Pax Christi, Campaign Against the Arms Trade, UNA, and other peace and human rights groups, he has been a Labour Party activist since 1987.

NORRIS McWHIRTER

The Freedom Association,
London SE1.

Dear Mr Kinnock,

I am one of those people whose involvement with the CND and unilateral nuclear disarmament probably goes back even further than Bruce Kent's – let alone yours. In April 1958, I took part in the first Aldermaston march. It was an experiment to see if people who advocate dismantling our defences nationally, are equally pacific when confronted with political opposition locally.

I soon had my answer: my car was attacked, its loudspeaker vandalised and its occupants kicked and punched by the marchers. Something similar happened 28 years later during the "second wave" of the CND.

Your party has been struggling with its pacifist tradition ever since its leader George Lansbury threatened to abolish our Armed Forces in 1933 – months after Hitler had become Chancellor of Germany. With the coming of nuclear weapons, this pacifist strand has become paradoxically aggressive, as I found out at Aldermaston.

In 1960, in his famous Scarborough Conference speech, Labour leader Hugh Gaitskell denounced what he rightly called 'the pacifists, unilateralists and fellow-travellers' who were forcing unilateralism upon his party. You have done nothing similar yourself, yet many commentators seem to think you have ditched unilateralism. I cannot see why they should believe this.

A recent article in the London *Evening Standard* credited a certain advertising executive with Labour's heavy defeat in the 1983 election. Positive presentation, it maintained, and a little help from General Galtieri, had been enough to win the day for the Conservatives. My memory of that campaign is very different. The main election issues were all negative: rising unemployment under the Conservatives, extremism in the Labour Party, and, above all, Michael Foot's determination to scrap all British nuclear weapons at the height of East-West confrontation.

You, too, will remember Labour's catastrophic election manifesto booklet – 'the longest suicide note in history', as it was appropriately dubbed. I was reminded of it when browsing through your party's so-called Policy Review document, *Meet the Challenge – Make the Change*, while preparing to draft this letter.

"Browsing" is hardly the right word, where no fewer than 88 pages of small print are concerned. One feels like an explorer trying to hack a path through impenetrable jungle.

Tucked away on page 87 is the following passage. Perhaps if it had not thus been buried in so wordy a document, its significance might have been better understood:

> Labour will immediately seek to place *all of Britain's nuclear capability* – including Polaris, and as much of Trident as has been completed – into international nuclear disarmament negotiations. The important objective of early decommissioning, first Polaris and then of Trident, could be pursued by Britain within the context of the START-2 [Strategic Arms Reduction Talks] negotiations, depending on their pace and progress. If the beginning of START-2 is subject to long delay, and there is good reason to believe that these negotiations will not make the progress we will require, a Labour government will reserve the option of initiating direct negotiations with the Soviet Union and/or with others *in order to bring about the elimination of that capacity by negotiated and verifiable agreements. Our aim is to bring about the elimination of that capability.*
>
> [*My italics.*]

In other – simpler – words, Labour's policy will be to *negotiate away* Britain's entire nuclear capability. In return for that, you hope to achieve some reduction in Soviet nuclear hardware. Instead of giving up everything for nothing, you will negotiate away everything in return for a fraction of the Soviet nuclear arsenal.

How can Labour claim to 'meet the challenge and make the change' in this way? Don't you remember how, before the 1983 election, Michael Foot accepted President Andropov's offer to give up a Soviet missile for every scrapped British missile? Can't you recall President Chernenko's similar offer to you in Moscow in 1984 which (as an avowed unilateralist) you were happy to accept? What difference does it make to our strategic situation if the Soviets give up a fraction of their arsenal whilst retaining the power to wipe us out once we have abandoned all of ours?

What Special Intelligence has your party, guaranteeing that Mr Gorbachev will remain permanently in office and that his more conciliatory policies will never be reversed? How do you square your policy of giving up everything in return for a fraction of the Soviet nuclear arsenal with repeated Gallup polls showing that nearly seven out of every ten voters want us to keep nuclear weapons as long as the USSR has them, and only about a quarter of the electorate opposes this? And, above all, why should your "new" policy – which would leave the Soviet Union with thousands of nuclear weapons and us with none – be described as anything other than one-sided (or unilateral) nuclear disarmament?

These are the key questions which you will have to answer if the electorate is to believe that the defence of Britain would be safe in Labour's hands.

You can't, they won't and it isn't.

Yours sincerely,

Norris McWhirter

NORRIS McWHIRTER
Chairman,
The Freedom Association.

Norris McWhirter, CBE, was co-founder with his twin brother Ross of *The Guinness Book of Records*, the world's all-time best-selling copyright book. Both twins were involved in numerous political campaigns on subjects including education, national defence, trade union power and broadcasting. Following the assassination of Ross McWhirter by IRA terrorists in the mid-1970s, Norris became a founder member of the Freedom Association and is currently its chairman.

PAUL OESTREICHER

Coventry Cathedral.

Dear Mr Kinnock,

As a child I fled with my parents from Hitler's Germany. I then had
the good fortune to grow up and study in New Zealand. For a little
more than 30 years I have chosen to make Britain my home. Would
I have served my children better by returning to my New Zealand
home or my German roots? As a priest I should know that there is
no escaping the consequences of original sin by a return to some
would-be paradise. As a student of politics I should have learnt
long ago that the art of government can never be more than the
craft of the possible.

To have lived through the last two decades of British politics
and, to a considerable extent, the demoralisation of British society,
has been and remains a painful experience. Believing that social
justice is a necessary ingredient of a tolerable society, an essential
objective of both domestic and foreign policy, I must reject the
immorality (as I perceive it) of much of Thatcherite rule. But even
more depressing were the amoral years of Harold Wilson's Britain,
that then led many (though never a majority) to vote for the frank
pursuit of self-interest. Today we reap the barren harvest of
Labour rule, with not so much as a principle to guide it, followed by
a rigidly principled, petit-bourgeois, English Tory autocracy. In
many ways, at the end of the 20th century, Britain is back at the end
of the 19th. Only now, without an Empire.

When Harold Wilson was elected, hopes were high. I now look
forward to a Labour election victory much more soberly – though
not as any kind of certainty. If I am right that the art of government
is the craft of the possible, then we stand at the brink of a period of
history in which a great deal is possible. But not without
imaginative vision. My prayer is that you and your colleagues will
dare to dream dreams and will share them with the people. Without
our perestroika, the outlook for our children is too bleak to
contemplate. I have no socialist utopias in mind. But to start with,
Britain's four nations becoming an integral part of a more-or-less
socially just Confederation of Europe, ecologically and globally
responsible, and committed to the universal elimination of all

weapons of mass destruction.

You and I first met on a CND platform in a northern town hall, Leeds I think. your speech greatly impressed me. Will the Labour Party give this young politician a chance, I wondered. It has. And would he learn to temper idealism with the realism that the exercise of power demands? You have. Too much so, perhaps, for the good of the people. Why go on sailing in Tory waters, if not Thatcherite ones, on matters of defence? Why on earth revert to the "independent" possession of nuclear weapons, even as interim wisdom, when a people's revolution in the other half of Europe has made a non-nuclear defence policy, proudly presented with conviction, a potential vote winner? Why dish up a half-baked European policy, leaving the moral high ground to Ted Heath, and not just the moral high ground but also the sane recognition that national sovereignty is a dated concept? Why not affirm English and Welsh and Bavarian and Slovak and Croatian pride and identity within a socially and economically healthy Europe? That Europe may also help to heal Ulster's wounds.

There is little hope if the Labour Party can do no more than follow, rather than lead public opinion into a new and demanding millenium. Why not embark with enthusiasm, in alliance with the Green movement, on a high profile policy of putting the care of our global environment – and therefore our survival – at the top of the agenda, and with it a radically new relationship with the nations of the two-thirds world? Why walk so warily when the times demand that we stride out boldly?

Why not take the Party by the scruff of the neck into this future, signalling where the nation will need to follow if its cities are to be healed; its poor reintegrated into society; its care for the sick and needy restored freely to all, young and old; its children educated to take pride in life and work, as they build the future?

All that is a 20 year programme – or more. But the spelling out needs to start now. Do not insult the people by assuming they cannot understand such a challenge and rise to it. Plan for power in 1991 or 1992, but better risk losing one more election than venture all on winning it by an appeal to no more than short term palliatives. Compromise is a political virtue. But without a vision there is nothing to compromise about. Mrs T's inability to compromise may lead to her political undoing. That will not be your problem. But it might be your opportunity and, just possibly, part of the fulfilment of our hopes.

Your agnosticism in matters spiritual is no stumbling block to me. I'm hopeful that my prayers will be no stumbling block to you.

Affectionately and in critical solidarity,

PAUL OESTREICHER.

Canon Paul Oestreicher is an Anglican priest and Quaker. He is Director of International Ministry at Coventry Cathedral. A Vice-President of CND, he was chairman of Amnesty International in Britain from 1974 to 1979. A graduate in political science, he has been a BBC producer and a parish priest but has mainly worked for the churches in international relations.

RON TODD

TGWU,
London SW1.

Dear Mrs Thatcher,

Like you I have a number of passionate convictions that have been with me practically all of my life, and like you, my desire to see change motivates me in my daily work. Whilst you believe that the unfettered free market should guide us, I am totally convinced that only through careful planning and regulation can we eradicate unnecessary evils such as unemployment, homelessness or low pay that plague our society.

But there is one thing that makes all of this seem secondary to me, one issue that casts a cloud over everything that we do; that is the threat of nuclear destruction.

As a consequence I have spent much of my life working for a world free from the nuclear threat. I have spoken at meetings and rallies, attended vigils and taken part in marches. I hope that I have done something to influence opinion. But I have not entered into this blindly. In the Royal Marines I played my part in fulfilling a role in protecting and serving Britain – I am not a pacifist, I know we need protection. But like millions of people throughout Britain, my fear is that our very protection will be the cause of our complete destruction.

Yet over the past eleven years your administration has done little to ease my fears. You have consistently isolated Britain in international negotiations. As the political map of Europe has changed you have avoided harmony between our European allies on the reduction of nuclear stockpiles. You have ignored the reductions the United States has made to its nuclear presence in Europe. And you have spurned the genuine attempts by the Soviet Union to create a climate where we can all prosper free from excessive military expenditure.

Instead for 11 years it has been the same story – Britain must be able to defend itself, independently if need be, against the nuclear threat – yet it is painfully clear that there is no defence against nuclear attack. Either a country is mad enough to use nuclear first strike capability, and in that case no form of defence will deter them. Otherwise a country can have nuclear weapons but never intend first use. I believe the latter just might be the case both in NATO and the Warsaw Pact, despite NATO deploying first use hardware – yet the only reason both sides maintain a nuclear strike capability is through fear that the other side may have superiority and use that superiority to either invade or destroy their opponent.

This form of mutual mistrust worked well for the militarists from 1945 to the mid 1980s. Then Mr Gorbachev came along and took the initiative. By making continued unilateral cuts in both conventional and nuclear forces in Eastern Europe he showed us that he was capable of rising above the paranoia that keeps the war chiefs and the arms suppliers of this world in business. And how did the West respond? Well at first there was disbelief that a Soviet leader could make unilateral cuts. Your mentor, Ronald Reagan ignored these developments and whilst he and you were happy to take the photocall opportunities with Mr Gorbachev, both you and Mr Reagan played the cold war out to the full, updating weaponry and building nuclear stockpiles big enough to destroy the world a hundred times over.

Fortunately, Mr Reagan is no longer President and a far more intelligent and pragmatic President is in power in America. George Bush realises that there is little future in excessive levels of nuclear capability and has agreed substantial reductions in the numbers of military personnel in Europe and the levels of cruise missiles in Britain. These actions are not unilateral in themselves, but they are in fact a positive response to Soviet arms reductions and political change in Eastern Europe. Yes Mrs Thatcher, Mr Bush has also taken some initiative and this must create difficulties for you – but then you and Mr Bush have had a few "difficulties" between you have you not? The days of the cosy relationship with an actor cum President cum actor are clearly over.

Recently the reunification of Germany has become a major issue. With reunification, the biggest country in Western Europe, the country at the very centre of the East/West divide, will now have to change its nuclear strategy. After all, a united Germany is not going to threaten the front line of the Eastern bloc when it happens to border East Germany itself. Thus the German people who overwhelmingly accept reunification, overwhelmingly reject nuclear weapons. Consequently another ally, Helmut Kohl, is forced to change position and reject nuclear defence. He is now no longer 'one of us', or should I say 'one of you'.

So Mrs Thatcher, you are left alone. Swept away by the tide of change in Europe both East and West. Despite these momentous events taking place throughout the world you refuse to yield and you have rejected the opportunity of playing a part in bringing these changes about. Because of this Britain no longer occupies the centre stage in world affairs. Of course it is not just in the sphere of arms cuts that you are out on a limb. You have also defied virtual unanimity on issues such as European financial and political union, sanctions on South Africa or the dumping of toxic wastes at sea.

Without doubt, Mrs Thatcher, you are an "iron lady", a woman not for turning. That arguably may have been seen as an admirable quality in the 1980s, but times change. As we move into the 1990s and look forward with excitement to the next century, leaders of the world will need other qualities. Compassion, understanding and care will be the watchwords of the future – words I am afraid I cannot associate with your time in office.

Yours sincerely,

[signature: Ron Todd]

RON TODD,
General Secretary,
Transport & General Workers' Union.

Ron Todd is General Secretary of the Transport and General Workers' Union. After working at Ford's from 1954 to 1962, latterly as Deputy Convenor, he became a full-time TGWU officer in 1962, becoming National Organiser in 1978, and a member of the TUC General Council in 1984. He is President of the Unity Trust, a member of the Council for Charitable Support, and an honorary Vice-President of CND.

BRIAN ALDISS

Oxford.

Dear Mrs Thatcher,

Ever since you became Prime Minister, you have exhibited strong nationalistic tendencies. The most notable manifestation of this trait was the unfortunate Falklands War. More recently, we have your negative attitude towards Europe and joining the EMS.

Agreed, these attitudes made you widely popular with the unthinking patriots in the country. I want to put forward an unpopular view, that patriotism carries heavy cash and ecological penalties in the modern world. I will quote on my side Dr Johnson, who described patriotism, you will recall, as the last refuge of a scoundrel.

We are all subject to what Jung labelled archetypes, compulsions that drive us against our intellect. Patriotism is a cocktail of two archetypes, aggression on the one hand, abasement on the other – an uneasy mix. When we declare we would die for England, or for Queen and Country, or however the boast is phrased, we are expressing aggression against whoever we believe the foe to be and submission, the bowing of the head, to authority at the same time.

These traits are observed in animals, even in the humble crayfish. They help propel the living world forward. But to encourage them in human beings is not desirable; that they are a part of the evolutionary mechanism does not make them welcome within society; rather, we might hope to educate them out. At present you have no such plans; rather, as I understand it, you are trying to narrow down history education in schools to a study of English history. The Boer War, for heaven's sake!

For the sake of brevity, I will curtail my argument and ask you to consider not the Boer but the Cold War, which we now believe – those of us who have no vested interest in NATO – to be over and buried. Throughout the weary years of the Cold War, patriotism was invoked on a wide scale. It appeared essential that Britain should keep an independent deterrent. Invocation of an external enemy excused many internal shortcomings in traditional fashion.

Now Mr Gorbachev has become one of the good guys. Russians are suddenly our friends. These switches in attitude take place overnight, as witness China – on, off, on, off. It's a mind game, fuelled by notions of "patriotism".

For all the horrifying manoeuvres of the Cold War, we were spared the great threat that paralysed our lives, that made us regard our children with loving despair, nuclear annihilation. I regard our survival as a fluke, rather than the outcome of good statesmanship. But how much has the Cold War cost?

Perhaps the total cost cannot yet be estimated; nor would anyone willingly undertake the task. I would surmise that it has cost more than any other hot war in history. Some items on the bill would be: the maiming and distorting of millions of lives repressed under the authoritarianism of war-footing; the spectacular diversion of funds from humanistic causes to all aspects of militarism; support given, often surreptitiously, to regimes good and bad and indifferent in the Middle East and Third World, in order that "little wars" might be fought as appendices to the main ideological struggle; the exploitation of poor countries for the same reason; the prodigal use of irreplaceable raw materials and fuels for useless weaponry and suchlike.

This list is by no means complete, but I will add only one more item: the ecological desecration of much of the planet.

Following the political confessions from the countries of the Warsaw Pact, we are receiving news of the Cold War's depredations on the environment. You will be familiar with the examples, exhibited like bleeding wounds on television, from Poland, Romania, Czechoslovakia, and elsewhere. Dying forests, dead lakes – these are the common currency of the world into which we are entering. In the Soviet Union, ecological catastrophes are legion. The death of the Aral Sea has the most far-reaching effects. Magnetogorsk, a town founded by Stalin to produce steel for tanks, is still using open-hearth furnaces of a type that went out here in Victorian times. Why? – Not just through the perversity of central planning (for which you seem to have an enthusiasm), but because Russia poured so much investment, better employed elsewhere, into keeping up with the West, maintaining its military stance.

Useless to ask now, Who's to blame? Patriotism is a very European disease, and ideology is its tertiary stage.

Many of these desperate hell-holes – one readily thinks of many more instances – are contributing to the overheating of the planet through the reckless burning of fossil fuels – the greenhouse effect. Your pose as a Green lacks credibility while your government plans ambitious new road systems instead of improving public transport services; the private automobile is a major polluter on a global scale. Patriotism certainly will not be best served by laying all of Britain under concrete, like a chillier Florida.

But to return to my main argument. However reluctantly, Western nations are now preparing to give aid and loans to the ruinous Central and Eastern countries of Europe they were only recently prepared to destroy...That is well enough. However, there are already signs that financing will be forthcoming in part by tapering off aid to the poorer countries of Africa and elsewhere. All this next instalment of misery must be added to the Cold War bill.

Patriotism now is not enough, if ever it was. I would like to see a statesman stand up and say that it is insufficient to love our country. That we should all love our planet. And that those fine words would be backed by a new and more generous system of education which would show us how best to go about it. And that the antagonisms of nationalism and ideology should somehow be subject to a greater understanding of human potential, and buried.

Do you know of such a statesman, Mrs Thatcher? I can't spot anyone of that ilk in our Parliament at present.

Yours unfaithfully,

[signature]

BRIAN ALDISS.

Brian Aldiss has enjoyed independence as a writer for over 30 years, though his career was once described as 'a course for commercial suicide'. He writes novels, short stories, and the science fiction for which he is best known. His autobiography, *Bury My Heart at W. H. Smith's*, appeared this year from Hodder & Stoughton. He is a Fellow of the Royal Society of Literature.

H. R. F. Keating is primarily a crime novelist, most of whose books are centred on Inspector Ghote of the Bombay CID. They have twice won the annual Gold Dagger award. A former Chairman of the Society of Authors, he was born in 1926. His latest book is *The Iciest Sin.*

H. R. F. KEATING

London W2.

Dear Neilgaret Thatchock,

Your victim addresses you. I doubt whether, even with the best intentions, you will read all of what I am about to write, or if you do whether what I say will stay with you for more than ten seconds. I realise you are convinced – you have to be – that matters of vital importance occupy your every waking hour, whether to spend another million pounds on a fighter plane, whether to dish out another ten or twenty million on the health service.

So you will hardly be prepared to take in that, to me, and I suspect to many thousands of others, all your decisions, all your debates, are as nothing. Whatever you choose to do, on our behalf, we know we have no say about it. We even lack the facts on which to judge the matters you have become the arbiter of. It is not your fault, I recognise, that this situation has come about. It has happened because of the monstrous complexity of the society we find ourselves living in.

So, though when the time comes I will probably vote for your party (and do so largely on the vague feelings I have about your own personality) I will go round to the polling-booth as much as anything for fun. I like races, I like an occasional gamble, and the Grand National doesn't come round quite often enough. I may at that time even begin to believe again that I have some influence on the future of the land in which I live. But that will be only the delusion of a moment. I know deep down that whichever party my one vote contributes to putting into power things will go on far above my head for the succeeding four of five years and nothing I do or say will truly alter that.

So what, assuming for one mad, unlikely moment you were to heed what I am telling you, would I like you to do? Resign? Come down and live like one of us, at the mercy of the whims and deep decisions of those we have elected to power? No point. If you were to step down, a hundred eager little feet would begin to trot towards your vacant pedestal. So stay there. Why not? It really makes little difference who stands on the plinth.

It's heresy to say so, but I am inclined to think that even if the pedestal were occupied by a Hitler or a Stalin, though certainly there would be more terrible things done than when your shoes stand up there, on balance for us down, down, down below life would not be all that different. There would be minuses, and there would be pluses. Some of us would be lucky (For some extraordinary reason at this moment I am being asked to pay much, much less than before for my local services while others I know are being asked to pay much, much more) and others would be unlucky. But nothing any of us can do would have more than the tiniest effect on our lives.

But this being at the mercy of swirling impersonal events (which you necessarily feel yourself to be more or less in charge of, rather than those young men in shirtsleeves we see on television shouting down telephones about millions of pounds, dollars and yen) is not confined to the issues which affect our country as a whole. The same thing happens at that local level where I am being suddenly asked to pay less. What influence have I had on that?

What influence can I have on any of the pettiest details of the life around me? Perhaps, just occasionally, if it transpires that a large number of my immediate neighbours have the same idea about some particular issue as I have, we can all band together, for a few weeks, for a month or two, and shout and shout and shout and eventually get a small change made. But here again it is really, in the complicated set-up that even a fairly small locality is enmeshed in nowadays, more a matter of luck, of pure chance than of there being any way in which I myself, vote hard as I like, can substantially alter things.

Well, there you are. Rule away, make mistakes, get some things right. But whatever you do or don't do I will just have to suffer it, or sometimes perhaps rejoice over it. But I know that, sing or squeak, I shall have had no say in all the mighty events you get under way. But carry on, carry on. There's nothing else you can do. And me? Well, I'll try to do what little I can to help my neighbour out of my own resources, by way of assistance, by way of example, by way occasionally of putting new thoughts into his head or hers. And maybe my little will actually be more beneficial in the end than your great. Who knows?

Yours (Yours indeed),

H. R. F. Keating

H. R. F. KEATING.

CHAD VARAH

St Stephen Walbrook,
City of London.

Dear Mrs Thatcher,

When you visited St Stephen Walbrook to see the Henry Moore altar, I had the opportunity to bless you. We both knew that this was nothing to do with party or policies, past, present or likely future. It was a recognition that a Christian bearing a heavy burden of responsibility has need of the grace of God, giving inward and spiritual strength. No one in this Realm, and few in this world, have greater responsibilities (and of course greater opportunities) than you, and it was a privilege to commend you to God in this holy place.

I did not lobby you then, and whatever other contributors to this book may choose to do, I shall not lobby you now. I shall merely urge you to emulate St Paul when he told King Agrippa (Acts 26, 19) that he was not disobedient to the heavenly vision. Or, to turn from the Bible to the Bard, 'To thine own self be true'. To follow our inner light is not easy for any of us, but I guess it is most difficult for a politician. It must be hard for anyone who can do nothing in public life without the votes of the wise and the foolish, the honest and the venal, the disinterested and those with vested interests, to resist the temptation to be 'all things to all men'. Perhaps a politician deserves to be called a statesman if he/she consistently refuses to use dubious means to supposedly good ends: who states 'here I stand; I can do no other'. Those who have, and want, no skill in hedging and trimming are called "obstinate". Well, if I were being pursued by a lynch mob, I'd be glad of some obstinate, awkward character who yelled 'Wait! Let's stop and make sure we're doing right before we do anything irreversible.'

You can be proud of being a lady who is not for turning, if by "turning" is meant 'being turned away from her principles by pressure from outside'. Being turned inwardly in one's convictions by the Holy Spirit is a different matter. I was brought up to believe that the highest virtue is the moral courage to stick to one's principles even if that attracts misunderstanding, misrepresentation and calumny. I despise unprincipled people and I respect those who (after reasoned debate) stick to principles with which I disagree.

I think I know what many of your basic principles are, and I want to refer to only one of these which is dear to my own heart: the principle that peoples with an established identity and a homeland have not merely the right, but the duty, to govern themselves. Most people would pay lip-service to this principle because they would be embarrassed to defend the opposite view, but only those of us who see the principle as an expression of the Divine Will can insist on giving it the highest priority. We are to use our time here on earth to become steadily more fit for heaven. We can make progress in this only by the moral choices we freely make. Any totalitarian system grievously reduces our free choices and may require us to make a choice which may be beyond our strength, namely to do evil at the behest of the State, or become martyrs. Democracy – making our own decisions – is the only right form of government for God's children, and the fact that some decisions may be mistaken or sinful does not invalidate this.

You have more power than I to assert and defend this principle, but even you cannot insist that it operate everywhere. What we can do is to state the principle firmly, whatever tyrant may be offended. You were able to see to it that Argentina did not capture the Falkland Islands. You will not let Spain annexe unwilling Gibraltarians. The struggle to prevent part of the United Kingdom of Great Britain and Northern Ireland from being incorporated into a neighbouring Republic continues. Sometimes we have been the evildoers: why did we ever put the Christian and animist south of Sudan at the mercy (inappropriate word) of the Muslim north, and why aren't we trying now to prevent the genocide there? Must the Eritreans and Tigreans be kept enslaved to Ethiopia? Will the Kurds ever be allowed Kurdistan, or the Basques have their little home astride the Franco-Spanish frontier? Why do the Azerbaijanis *wish* to govern the Armenians of Nagorno-Karabakh, or the Romanians the Hungarians of Transylvania? Have the Indonesians no shame about the peoples who do not wish to be ruled by them? In Brazil, how many votes are the Yanomami and other threatened Indian peoples worth?

You are bold as well as scientifically "green". Will you not address, before it is too late, blistering words to the government of Malaysia, whose Minister for Forests (of all people) has granted to the family of the Minister for the Environment (of all people) logging concessions in Sarawak which are destroying an irreplaceable virgin forest and the gentle Penan people who inhabit it, making millions by selling the looted hardwoods to the Japanese, whose wastefulness is demonstrated by their throwing away two billion wooden chopsticks a week?

The China to which we engaged to return the New Territories of Hong Kong (not, I'm told, Victoria and Kowloon) in 1997 no longer exists, unless in Taiwan. So why do we not call a halt to the handing over of the whole of Hong Kong to the country which ruthlessly annexed Tibet long before the massacre in Tiananmen Square? We may be helpless before the biggest powers, but must we be shamefully silent? As I write these words, Mr Bush, Monsieur Mitterand, and Herr Kohl are rejecting Lithuania's 'Munich' gibe and taking the view (as *The Times* expresses it) that 'Lithuanian freedom has a lower priority than Mr Gorbachev's survival, Soviet internal reform and international arms reductions'. Not in my book, it doesn't. *Fiat justitia, ruat coeli.* The USSR has at long last admitted the massacre of Katyn. Those Polish officers get no benefit. *Living* Lithuanians, Latvians and Estonians have a right to be told: 'The evil Stalin agreed with the evil Hitler that your countries should be forcibly incorporated into the Soviet Union: please now consider yourselves free, and let us see if in any way we can work together.'

Yours most sincerely,

CHAD VARAH.

Prebendary Dr Chad Varah, OBE, MA (Oxon.), is Rector of the Lord Mayor's Parish Church of St Stephen Walbrook in the City of London, where he founded The Samaritans in 1953 and Befrienders International in 1974. He is an Honorary Fellow of Keble College, Oxford, and was made an Honorary LLD. by Leicester University. He holds the Albert Schweitzer Gold Medal 'for inspiring the world's youth in the service of humanity'. From 1950 to 1962 he was Scripwriter for *Eagle* and *Girl.*

LEO ABSE

London W4.

Dear Mrs Thatcher,

I have taken the precaution of marking the envelope 'Please forward' since, by the time you have received this note, it is just possible you may have moved to Dulwich: but I do hope this will find you still at Downing Street since you will only have changed your address either because you have retreated into a psycho-somatic illness – a common enough escape route of many a failed maniac political leader – or been displaced by Heseltine. I do not wish such disasters on you or on the nation: it will politically be more therapeutic that your disaster is the consequence of the democratic process at the next general election.

Now, once again, I have to overcome the diffidence which embarrasses me when I write of you or to you. After all, so many years of my life have been spent, as a penal reformer or defending lawyer, extenuating the grievous offences of the anti-social, the murderers, rapists and gangsters; and always the mitigation I have pleaded is the essential involuntariness of their conduct. Their deviancy, as yours, was shaped by their sad inheritance: their destiny was usually determined not only genetically but also, above all, by their earliest tragic family environment.

You, likewise, endured similar early disadvantages. You were brought up within a bleak household where frivolity was forbidden, where play was frowned upon, holidays rarely taken, and where the only intermission from money making in the grocery shop, above which you lived in comfortless rooms, was constant visits to a chapel governed by a particularly puritanical brand of narrow sectarian Protestantism where the work ethic of the English petty bourgeoisie was preached. My theory is that the real altar of your family was the till, for the greed enveloping it was pathological: although by no means poor, your moderately successful shopkeeper father never even installed for you an inside lavatory or a bathroom.

Yet perhaps the most grievous deprival you suffered was not material but emotional: you were unlucky enough to be born to a cold affection-less mother, herself dominated by the cold living-in controlling martinet of a mother. The hostility you felt to your unloving mother left you with little alternative but manically to deny you were in any way dependent upon her. How could you bear to acknowledge dependency upon someone whom you would wish to obliterate from memory? And this pattern of your childhood is irrevocably embossed upon your adult character: irrationally you attempt to erase your mother from your biography, an effort which has had awesome public consequences.

This hatred and fear of dependency has provided you with the dynamic to assault the Welfare State: every succouring institution, the health and social services, all are subliminally perceived by you as mother surrogates. Everyone must stand on his own two feet: no individual, no region, should receive aid: there must be no such thing as society, for that is founded on interdependence, an emotional condition which you are fated never to be able to tolerate.

Functionally, it may well be that Britain had become insufficiently self-reliant and a corrective may have been needed to ward off the inimical effects of a dependency culture, but you are not able to make a cool appraisal, balancing the need to support the disadvantaged against the hazards of quenching individualistic vigour. You are not, in fact, a woman in control in the driving seat: you are a driven woman, and your personal needs have been elevated to an ideology. To maintain your personal defences, you have no alternative but to go on and on: you are compelled to be heedless of the warnings within your Party to go slower, to consolidate. You cannot apply the brakes for, as the electorate increasingly understands, you are off your trolley.

Lamentably, when you are forced to quit, the excesses of Thatcherism, like those of Stalinism in Eastern Europe, will have discredited all ideology. But to eschew theory, to mock at idealism and to equate it with illusory millenarianism, is to hand over government to the technocrat. The triumph of the technocrat would mean the end of moral exhilaration in our public affairs. Politics would be no art: the politician would proffer to the electorate not inspiration but only his managerial skills.

Already your excesses have left the door open for such a man to displace you. Heseltine is a technocrat who belongs to that dangerous group of politicians who cast themselves as their own hero. At Oxford he was known as Michael Philistine and there he was ever lured to the cinema to find the cowboy heroes with whom he could identify. Gary Cooper was his pseudonym, High Noon was his favourite hour. When the clock strikes Tarzan Heseltine swings into action, holds up the mace and fearlessly, before the cameras, strides out of the Cabinet. Heseltine to the Rescue is the title of all his productions. Westland Helicopter Group, Merseyside and now the Conservative Party. But all the rescues are to be achieved by managerial skills. His ability as Secretary of State for Defence was that of the technocrat; protected by his unimaginativeness he was at ease in dealing with the technicalities of terrible modern weaponry and missilery.

And meantime, too, my Party is in danger of over-reacting to your doctrinal extravagance. Modernising the Party by jettisoning anachronistic ideology may be necessary, but stripping it of all political philosophy, in order to demonstrate how, unlike you, we are pragmatists, could reduce us to a party of technocrats. If your legacy is to leave Britain fearful, cynical or even suspicious of political idealism then that will have been your worst disservice, for politics will be demeaned if the electorate is only able to choose between rival professional managerial groups of technocratic legislators. This is not inevitable: nothing in politics is, but it does mean you unwittingly have set us romantics a hard task to ward off the danger. But we must try.

Yours sincerely,

Leo Abse

LEO ABSE.

Leo Abse is a lawyer, social reformer and psychobiographer. As a Labour MP from 1958 to 1987 he was responsible for more Private Members' Acts than anyone this century; these Acts included radically altering laws relating to divorce and homosexuality. His psychobiography, *Margaret, Daughter of Beatrice*, was published by Cape in 1989.

D. M. Thomas is a novelist, poet and translator. His novels include *The White Hotel* (shortlisted for the Booker Prize), *Summit*, and most recently, *Lying Together* (Gollancz, 1990). He divides his time between writing and tutoring poetry and fiction courses at his house in Cornwall.

D. M. THOMAS

Truro, Cornwall.

Dear Mrs Thatcher,

I imagine this book of letters will be full of abuse from deck-chair Socialists, and I have no intention of adding to it. Instead I would like to congratulate you on your premiership. Although your touch seems to have deserted you of late – temporarily, I hope – I think you have been an excellent Prime Minister.

You taught us the hard lesson that a country, like a family, has to live within its means. Your voice has been free from cant, sociological jargon and windy rhetoric.

You have brought a more human, feminine touch to our politics. Oh, of course, your royal We is irritating, and I wish you'd learn to say I; but at crucial moments, like the Falklands and the Brighton bombing, you haven't been afraid to show your feelings in a way somehow impossible for male politicians.

You have been a great friend to democracy, both at home and abroad. At home, you curbed the undemocratic Union barons; and you have forced the Labour Party to democratise itself: one of your finest achievements may turn out to have been the creation of a decent alternative to your own party. Abroad, you helped – with understandable reluctance – to bring to birth an African kind of democracy in Rhodesia. Without your firmness over the Falklands, Argentina would today still be a military dictatorship. And through your friendship with, and encouragement of, Mr Gorbachev you have contributed greatly to the liberation from Communism of Eastern Europe. Few statesmen or women – I think you would shudder, as I do, at statesperson – have helped democracy so well.

Speaking of democracy, I am not aware that anyone has ever asked me if I wish to be a citizen of a federal Europe. Indeed, when the referendum took place, I was assured this would never occur. As it happens, I hate the idea of European federation. If Britain votes for it, I would have to accept it, but I object to the present bullying and browbeating (of you) when the electorate has had no chance to express its wishes. So all power to you in your caution and "stubbornness".

By the way, I write as someone who is not a Conservative, nor a

Socialist, nor a Liberal Democrat – but a floating voter; that is to say, I am quite proud of having a free mind. I certainly don't agree with everything you have done. I wish you were more sceptical about big business and military power. With the privatisation of water and electricity, and with the Poll Tax, I think you have let ideology overcome common sense and pragmatism. My hope for the nineties is that you will re-discover your popular touch, give ideology a rest, help Russia all you can, and fight to preserve our independence within a Europe of friendly nations – from Ireland to the Urals. I hope you will find it possible to reduce military expenditure considerably, and with the money saved improve the health service and the environment. And on a personal level I'd like you to develop a more relaxed style, and reveal the warm human being that I am sure you really are.

Thank you, finally, for giving me the enormous pleasure of seeing most of my literary friends and acquaintances grow apoplectic with fury at the mere sound of your name. I know you have had a pseudo-Freudian analysis written about you; I think the unconscious of your attackers is more worthy of serious Freudian study. I doubt if they would feel as virulent towards a male Prime Minister who had fought his way up from a corner grocer's shop and Grammar School. (I am tempted to leave my mistyping there: 'fought his wife up' – a good Freudian joke, no?)

Of course, the hostility of the *intelligentsia* is almost a guarantee that you have been doing okay; since they are mostly the kind of people who would have turned Communist and lauded Stalin in the thirties, and clamoured for negotiations with Hitler. Nevertheless, their attacks must sometimes hurt, and I think your stamina under fire has been admirable.

One consolation must be the sure knowledge that in 20 years' time, long out of power, you will become an affectionately-regarded institution, like the Queen Mother or some ageing Wimbledon ladies' tennis champion. I hope you will write a stunningly honest autobiography, including your real feelings for your parents and your love-life. I look forward to reading it – but not for a few years yet.

Yours sincerely,

D. M. THOMAS.

MICHAEL BLACKBURN

Lincoln.

Dear Mrs Thatcher,

Well, I've been turning this letter over in my head, making drafts in verse and prose, wondering what to say and how to say it and asking myself if I'll just be repeating what a lot of others have said.

It hardly seems worth worrying about since you've always made it quite plain that no one else's opinions are worth listening to, and that you are always right and everyone else is wrong. I sometimes wonder if you think reality itself is wrong. Can your condition be clinically defined? Downing Street Bunkeritis, perhaps?

You played on the lowest common denominators to get into power and stay there: on the desire for personal gratification without public responsibility; on the love of wealth, not just for its power over others but for its specious claim to moral superiority; on a braying nationalism whose tactless ignorance in diplomatic circles is matched by the brutality of football hooligans abroad; and on fear – fear of being left behind in a race for essentials, fear that unless you dump your long-held values and beliefs you'll end up jobless, homeless, pensionless, doctorless.

I resent being taken for a fool that I cannot see, for instance, that state power is more centralised and unaccountable than before; that wealth is not more evenly, more justly distributed than before; that unemployment, poverty and squalor have not been done away with but actually intensified; that the much-vaunted doctrine of individualism has led to a stifling personal and social conformism.

The whole saga is really rather sorry. And now, to cap it all, as they say, the Poll Tax Fiasco. If anything exemplifies the madness, injustice and plain incompetence of your administration, this does. Whoever thought this one up deserves having his head examined and then removed.

In the end, everything about you is a bit tacky, isn't it? All those clever slogans from your admen and advisers; the regal manner on the one hand and the little-wifey-with-the-handbag on the other; the unctuous insincerity of your elocution. I often despaired of my own compatriots: how could they fall for this charade? It's a pity that our wonderful "democratic" system can transform a forty per cent voting minority into an unrepresentative parliamentary majority.

In addition, though, I have a greater faith in the British people, whatever their race, creed or colour; a faith in their compassion, tolerance, generosity and sense of justice. These are virtues to foster and strive for, not to sneer at and deride, as the ethos of the past eleven years would have us do. Maybe I'm just old-fashioned, but my instinct as well as my intelligence tells me that those who 'drivel and drool' about such things as the National Health Service are better people to live among than those whose first loyalty is to their wallet.

I remember watching you on TV on an early campaign trail. You were in a tea factory, pretending to be interested in the workers. They showed you how they tested the blends by taking a spoonful of neat tea and swilling it around the tongue before spitting it out. They said you had to spit it out because it was too bitter to swallow. You, of course, knew better. Spitting, even in the course of professional duty, was a disgusting practice that no lady could be seen to do in public. So you swallowed your spoonful. It must have been bitter – your face crumpled up like a paper bag. Serves you bloody right, I thought. There was more revealed about you in that brief encounter than in a thousand appearances on *Wogan*.

The nation has had to suffer eleven years of enforced bitterness, to no benefit. No one knows how many more years it will take to purge itself of its poisonous effects. I have no qualms, therefore, in saying that my disgust and contempt for what you stand for and what you have done are absolute and unqualified.

When you eventually emerge from the Downing Street Bunker, it won't be with glory. But I shouldn't think that will bother you. You'll probably go to the grave believing you did this country a favour.

Thanks for nothing.

Yours implacably,

M. A. Blackburn

MICHAEL BLACKBURN.

Michael Blackburn is a poet, writer, and editor of *Sunk Island Review*. He works as a Literature Animateur, setting up literary events and encouraging people of all ages and backgrounds to take up creative writing. His poetry collections include *Backwards into Bedlam* and *The Lean Man Shaving*.

PETER LEVI

Frampton on Severn,
Gloucestershire.

Dear Mrs Thatcher,

I am not a member of your party, and since I have recently moved from Douglas Hurd's constituency to a remoter spot, where I seem to be represented in Parliament by a person I have never heard of, and whose party is a mystery to me, I shall not be taking much part in politics.

All the same, there are some things that worry me. I voted in favour of your honorary degree at Oxford and think it a shame it was never conferred; I have tried to stir up enthusiasm for a large bronze statue of you to decorate the Science area, which could be commissioned I believe without the nonsense of a popular vote, but I am told that even the bust of you in your old college has to be kept behind iron bars for its better protection. Ah well, that is politics, you will say. Still, it is sad, and it would not have happened in Harold Wilson's time.

You have observed the awful squealing of the privileged in university life as the belt begins to pinch, and you have properly ignored them, so that they are now at last raising money for themselves. But you have been forced to accept a quasi-equality among subjects and institutions which is really a fantasy, a kind of malign committee politeness, and to accept the idea that universities have "customers". In the present unhappy confusion, it is not surprising that university teachers are unhappy, but on the whole their claim to a divine right to infinite funding is insufferable, and you have been courageous to squash it.

You will soon be leaving politics, and I hope you may do so while you and Mr Thatcher, of whose fan-club I am a very early member indeed, can enjoy yourselves for some easy years. I would not personally have relished that house in Dulwich, and I do not expect we share a taste in ornaments, but you will be rich enough to travel as you like. I would be happy to recommend a decayed spa in France or Yugoslavia, a Greek hide-out approachable only from the sea, or a farmhouse near the Pyrenees with excellent local architecture, but I am not sure whether you would like these places, which I like. So may I invite you here to tea? We would celebrate your retirement, and your husband's emergence from the shadows. I have thought for some years that he should be your successor, the nation would vote for him with enthusiasm, since all those who truly support you like him twice as much. But the House of Commons is not a very desirable club; it entails being associated with the scum of the earth, and I would not wish membership on my worst enemy.

That makes it hard to take part in politics of course, and I have no pretension to do so except in national emergencies. (I must say we are quite close to one). My letter therefore must remain social. You have deserved well of your country, you are our first woman Prime Minister, and our first Prime Minister of distinctly lower middle-class origins. I applaud your achievements, and I congratulate you on many actions I don't now remember. Do come to tea.

Yours sincerely,

Peter Levi

PETER LEVI.

Peter Levi is a poet, translator, classical scholar and Hellenist. He joined the Society of Jesus in 1948, and was ordained as a priest in 1964, resigning in 1977 to marry Cyril Connolly's widow, Deirdre Craig. He has been a Fellow of St Catherine's College, Oxford, since 1977, and was Oxford Professor of Poetry from 1984 to 1989. His most recent books include an autobiography, *The Flutes of Autumn*; a novella, *To the Goat*; a verse lecture, *Goodbye to the Art of Poetry*; *The Life and Times of William Shakespeare*; and a biography of *Boris Pasternak*.

Auberon Waugh is the Editor of *Literary Review*. He also writes regular columns in the *Daily Telegraph* and *Spectator*. He has written five novels and ten non-fiction books. His best book yet is *A Turbulent Decade*, a second volume of *Private Eye* Diaries, but he has great hopes for his autobiography, *The First Fifty Years*, to be published by Hutchinson in 1991.

AUBERON WAUGH

Combe Florey,
Somerset.

Dear Mrs Thatcher,

Ever since the Gibraltar shootings on 6 March 1988 I have been urging you to retire gracefully from politics before it was too late. That incident convinced me you were no longer a fit person to have responsibility for maintaining law and order in Ulster against the murderers and terrorists of the IRA and UDF. Since then the case for a dignified retirement has grown by leaps and bounds.

Perhaps the most cogent reason for getting out while the going is good is that the great majority of the electorate is fed up with you, and is not going to elect another government under your leadership. The return of a socialist government under Kinnock and Hattersley would be a major national disaster, from which the country would almost certainly never recover. Your obstinacy is to blame for the fact that you are so much disliked, more than any sudden national revulsion. Poll Tax may have seemed a good idea, but as soon as the government discovered it was electorally and administratively unviable, you should have dropped it like a hot potato.

However, quite apart from the crippling electoral liability you now represent for the Conservative Party, there are signs that you are leading the country on the rocks of isolationism and industrial collapse by your attitude to the proposed EC integration of 1992. While all the countries of Europe propose to celebrate this event with open frontiers, harmonised excise duties and aligned currencies, you plan to keep Britain inside closed frontiers (for fear of the free movement of terrorists and drugs, you say) with its own nanny-system of punitive duties on alcohol and tobacco (because anything else would be a 'nightmare') and our own independent currency vulnerable to every assault from international speculators.

In all these things you are wrong. You have done many of the things which needed doing. Thank you. Now you are doing nothing but harm. Please go away.

Yours sincerely,

Auberon Waugh

AUBERON WAUGH.

CHRISTOPHER LOGUE

Worthing.

A POSTCARD FROM WORTHING

Dear Margaret and Neil,
The sea says nothing. The sea is bored.
"Who authorised you to speak for the sea?"
It did. It appeared in my sleep. It said:
"I have appeared to millions in their sleep.
No one will speak for me. Speak."
And who am I to disobey the sea?

confident that I will see you both soon,
yours,

chris.

Christopher Logue is a poet, translator, dramatist, actor, and a regular contributor to *Private Eye*. His latest book is *Kings: An Account of Books 1 and 2 of Homer's Iliad*, due to be published by Faber in 1991.

STAN BARSTOW

Ossett,
West Yorkshire.

Dear Mr Kinnock,

I have to start with a confession: though I have never voted Conservative in my life, there has nearly always been the odd Tory minister or shadow for whom I could feel some respect. I mean until the last few years, when Mrs Thatcher has remade them all in her own repugnant image. Now I detest them all.

How is it that the defeat of the Sandinista Government, who won 42% of the popular vote, by a coalition of opposition parties, is hailed as a victory for democracy in Nicaragua, while the massive majority enjoyed by the Tory Party with little more of our vote is seen as democracy at work in the Mother of Parliaments? When Tory MPs are too craven to oppose the government in measures with which they disagree, is it any wonder that the frustration of the people leads them on to the streets to demonstrate?

With our present electoral bias, what unimaginable swing would be needed to put Labour in the same commanding position?

Well, Labour had a spanking majority in 1945, but it didn't last long, and what I am about to advocate would mean that such a majority would never again be achieved by any party. I'm talking about proportional representation. To talk as the Left does of Labour going to the country with 'real Socialist policies' and expecting to win is moonshine. Too many people remember 1979 and the ease with which a Labour administration can be brought to grief. They know the Left to be dishonest. It cannot make its brand of socialism work voluntarily (because it's the biggest pig who gets most out of the trough) and who wants the other kind which is being dismantled all over Eastern Europe?

Proportional representation in the Labour manifesto would mean certain victory. (Which is the fairest method can be debated.) It would also lead to consensus and a relief from the kind of impotent fury one is beset by every day this present government retains power and goes on damaging our nation irreparably.

Consensus. We must find it before our people become divided in tragedy. Time is running out.

With every good wish,

Yours sincerely,

Stan Barstow

STAN BARSTOW.

Stan Barstow is a novelist and dramatist. His novels include *A Kind of Loving* and *Joby*, which is widely read in schools. He is currently writing the third novel in his Ella Palmer trilogy, following on *Just You Wait and See* and *Give Us This Day*. He also writes for radio and television, and is an Honorary MA of the Open University.

ELIZABETH WILSON

London NW5.

Neil –

By the time you read this letter I shall be far away, because, my dearest, I've realised that the only honest thing is for us to part. This hasn't been an easy decision – after all, we've been together since I was nineteen years old. But, darling, I think it has to be. For one thing, I've realised that I'm just no good to you. I read the other day that there are only a tiny seven per cent of people like me in the country – seven per cent of us who think of ourselves as "substantially" or "far" left. I'm old-fashioned, Neil, and set in my ways – you're destined for higher things, and I just wouldn't fit into your new life of pink thatcherism. Truly, darling, I'm an embarrassment to you. And in fact, I have sometimes felt recently that you were taking me rather for granted. When I went a bit green after I got ecology poisoning last summer I don't think you even really noticed. And I soon got over that anyway.

Our relationship is dead, Neil, can't you see that? It isn't as if you'd slept around – perhaps that would have been easier to understand in a way; it's just that we don't seem to have much in common any longer. Sometimes I almost wonder if you really meant all those things you used to say – about the kind of life we were going to have together. Of course I know you still hate to see beggars in the streets and it's a shame about unemployment and all that talk there used to be about soaking the rich was a bit over the top I suppose, but – Neil, just what *do* you believe in? Okay, it was charitable of you to offer Gran the use of the garden shed, but once upon a time you promised her a whole flat of her own.

Oh, I know my vote still counts for something, but the more I think about it, the more I'm even beginning to think that it's really only out of charity that you keep on accepting that. Admit it – be realistic; my vote's as embarrassing as the mufflers Granny used to knit you before her arthritis got so bad.

Was it all talk, Neil? I can't bear to think that, because I did believe in you, you know. Or rather, I believed, and still believe, in the hopes I thought we shared. Together we really could make some changes. And, Neil, I still think those changes need to be made – these days, you just talk about helping the poor as if we were Lord and Lady Bountiful, but I thought we were committed to building a society of equals in which there wouldn't be poor people any more. What happened to the irreversible shift in wealth and power? Oh, I know – now you just laugh and let those new friends of yours tell you how suicidal all that was.

But I don't want to blame your new friends – that's a bit cheap, really, isn't it? And I don't want to blame the times we live in either. Perhaps if we'd been stronger earlier on, things wouldn't have reached this stage – but – oh no, the odds were always stacked against us.

As I said, it isn't as if you'd exactly been unfaithful – and yet – I have to say it Neil, I didn't want to, believe me I didn't, but although you say you hate That Woman – well, however many rude things you say about her, there's no getting away from the fact that you've slavishly imitated everything she's done – everything, that is, except her radicalism. They say that imitation is the sincerest form of flattery – well, you've given her all the flattery while I've been left high and dry with nothing to look forward to and no one to turn to. I wonder if you realise just how bitter that makes me feel? You've nagged and nagged me to be more respectable, and yet *She's* not respectable at all. The New Respectability has just made you all inhibited – no thrust, no power – and where does that leave me? I wanted my man to have *convictions*, Neil – after all, that's the secret of Her success. I've never cared about tidy suits and ties, and do you know, I honestly don't think that a lot of people are as impressed by all that as you imagine.

And another thing, Neil. You've always confused criticism with lack of loyalty – and perhaps I was too critical. But I was loyal in my own way as well. Although I would never actually marry you, I did work for you, Neil, I canvassed, I spoke, I handed out leaflets, I – but, well, what's the use. I never could really make you understand...and now I guess I never will.

I don't know what else there is to say, really. This has been one of the most difficult letters I've ever had to write, because I don't want to hurt you, believe me I don't. But – this is the end, Neil. One thing, though – there's no one else. I promise you that. I never for a moment fancied David or David or Paddy – I never ever really even had a tiny little weird feeling about Sara, or only for a minute. But that's what makes it so hard – do you see. I really haven't anywhere else to go. I guess that's why I've stayed so long, hoping, always hoping that things were going to get better. Instead of which they've just got worse and worse, until now I can't really bear you to touch me (and I clearly turn you *right* off anyway) because it only reminds me of the way things might have been.

I expect I'll end up hanging out with all the unsuitable friends you never really liked (I see that now). The rabble – the gays, the anarchists, the too-extreme feminists, they always embarrassed you, I see it more and more clearly even as I'm writing this letter – but at least they stand for an *alternative* set of social values, some of them are clones, but at least they're not Tory clones.

I wish I felt this letter would do some good, Neil. But I can see you reading it and thinking – if she wants to marginalise herself, that's her arrogance, her stupidity. Because it's always been me who's been arrogant, who's been in the wrong – isn't it? You've always blamed me for what went wrong. I don't think you've ever faced up to your own arrogance, to the possibility that you too could be wrong from time to time.

And almost at once you'll feel relieved, because I wasn't smart enough for you, didn't say the right things, had this bohemian idea about not being married, and read too many books. No – believe me, it's for the best –

So – what more is there to say – except – THIS IS GOODBYE, NEIL, THIS TIME I REALLY MEAN IT.

I only hope to God you know what you're doing.

Yours,

[signature]

ELIZABETH WILSON.

Elizabeth Wilson is Professor of Sociology at the Polytechnic of North London. A feminist, communist and activist in the lesbian and gay movement, she is the author of a number of books, including *Adorned in Dreams*, *Hallucinations*, *Mirror Writing* and (forthcoming) *The Sphinx in the City*.

Henry Livings is a dramatist. His best-known play is probably *Eh?*, which was presented by the Royal Shakespeare Company and later became the show that first brought Dustin Hoffmann to public notice at the Circle in the Square, New York, where it won Livings an OBIE Award. He has published two books of short stories, *Pennine Tales* and *Flying Eggs and Things*, and lives on the edge of the Pennines outside Oldham with two lurcher dogs and a bad cough.

HENRY LIVINGS

Delph,
Oldham, Lancashire.

Dear Glenys (and hallo to Neil by this same),

A great number of us in the Labour Movement have trouble coming to terms with politics. The Right has no such problem, because they don't want to come to terms with politics in the first place; they like their authority, and the morality of money is, in their heads, unimpeachable. A number of tyrannical regimes tumble in Eastern Europe, and this is seen as the defeat of socialism by the Right; so we socialists have to pussyfoot round the word, hijacked in the service of unfettered money; because they say it frequently, therefore socialism has failed.

We're just as bad ourselves, the Movement is peppered with berks who think that To Do Good is socialist. Save a badger, stop the working man from catching rabbits, sabotage the Hunt, that, to them, is socialist. Big Jim Rostron, bricklayer extraordinaire, says he never yet saw a politician with a hod on his shoulder; his politics is 'if it works, it's socialist'; knowing Big Jim is like eating a trumpet while listening to caviare.

One other quote, this time from the President of the Association of Chartered Accountants, well he was, once: 'Profit without service,' he said, 'is theft.' Big Jim would call that socialism too. I wonder how we rescue socialism from obloquy? Possibly by making sure it works? Nationalisation didn't work all that well did it? I worked for British Rail just after it was created, and it was grievous to watch the bureaucracy moving in, wrecking working relationships between management and waged, by making grand overall decisions that didn't apply in the shunting yard. Not socialism for sure, more like state capitalism.

Good luck, you'll have it all to do when he's Prime Minister; he'll be far too busy to think, so now's the time.

Yours in brotherly affection,

Henry Livings

HENRY LIVINGS.

JONATHAN RABAN

F I R̶S̶T̶ CLUB

class

BA 293, LHR – Miami.

Dear Mrs Thatcher,

For ages now (nearly eleven years) I've been meaning to drop you a thank-you note; but have been so busy that only now, 33,000 feet up somewhere over the Atlantic, do I find myself with the necessary hour or so of leisure.

As you'll see from the letterhead, I'm flying Club Class, and the great achievement of your administration, as I see it, is to have made the world a nicer place for those of us who fly Club.

You can imagine the scene up here. The champagne trolley (Heidsieck Brut) has been busying up and down the aisle; we've just lunched (seafood and king crab terrine, followed by sautéed breast of Guinea fowl with Pear William). We look a generally well-fed bunch. The men among us (and men outnumber women five to one in Club Class) seem to suffer from a disproportionate amount of hair-loss, but otherwise it's all gain. We're plump, we dress in natural fabrics, we sport Cross 20-carat gold ballpoints, credit-card-size calculators, and on our wrists we exhibit the kind of watches whose brand-name you are meant to spot at a glance. My own is typical. It's a Dunhill – not quite a first class Patek-Philippe, but a cut and a half above the Timexes back in Economy.

Even during this 9¼-hour interval between continents, most of us are still working; like the guy in the seat next to mine (he's something in the aluminium business I gather), who's been leafing through a stack of faxes and is now taking pot-shots at a Hewlett-Packard vest-pocket computer with his forefinger.

Our faces are, on the whole, fleshy, pink and untroubled. We're aloof from worries about our Poll Tax or our mortgage repayments. High interest rates may be a problem to the chaps in Club Class if they've just invested in a lot of new industrial plant – but writers, thank heaven, don't need much in the way of plant to keep the wheels of their industry turning. We're aloof, too, about the cost of our air tickets (LHR-Miami return is £1858), because most of us haven't had to reach into our own pockets to fork out the fare. I'd say that we were a pretty average bunch of £50,000 p.a. men.

We're Club, not First. Our accents are mostly Midland, Yorkshire and suburban Essex. Eleven years ago, I doubt if many of us guessed that we'd be where we are today. I certainly didn't.

We feel a special debt to you. Your governments, with their stress on enterprise and incentives, on low income tax and mortgage-relief for homeowners, have done a lot to help us join the Club Class; and that alone would merit a thank-you letter.

But you have done much, much more. Like most of the forty-going-on-fifty men here in the cabin, I grew up in a guilty world. People who had wealth preferred to underplay it. They went around in old clothes and had watches that were just watches. The war had had a lot to do with it, of course. On the Normandy beaches, people from First, Club, Economy – and even the poor saps who are so lazy that they'll never afford the price of an air ticket of any class to anywhere, found themselves all in each other's company and discovered, on the battlefields as in the bombed cities at home, that a natural human kinship existed between them.

So, after the war, a lot of people in First and Club voted against their own class interests because they actually cared about the welfare of people in Economy. They even cared about the welfare of the non-fliers.

You've changed all that. You've made us understand, at last, that if some Bri-nylon-clad prole back there in Economy is squashed into a too-narrow seat with no legroom (our seats have recliners and comfortable foldaway leg rests), has eaten a far worse lunch than ours, hasn't had a sniff at the complimentary champagne or been pampered with a succession of warm damp towels, then it is his own damned fault. The poor booby simply doesn't deserve to travel as we do.

So the very thought of Economy (we are discreetly curtained-off from their envious view) makes us feel good. Our privileges are earned. They are our right. We "pity" the mugs in Economy, but feel no pity. Their numbers, their awful shirts, their cheap watches, serve only to bolster our self-esteem.

You've exposed the sham of bleeding-heart liberalism for what it is – an unnecessary waste of concern for people who ought to be

looking after themselves as we in Club Class look after ourselves. I
felt guilty once (heavens, I used to be Treasurer of a ward in the
Islington Labour Party in the soggy 1970s), but now I'm in Club
Class, and guiltlessly proud of it. I owe a lot of that to you. One
always feels strangely without weight at this altitude, but, you know,
Club Class people feel that weightlessness even when they're on
the ground. They feel *lighter*, and the weight that has been taken off
their shoulders is that old-fashioned and needless guilt, embarrassment and shame which used to afflict so many people like us
before you came to power.

That is something that you should take a great and just pride in.
'Lighten our hearts, we beseech thee, O Lord' says the prayer-
book. I can't tell how much you, by your teaching and your personal
example, have lightened the hearts of Club Class people like us.

With many thanks,

Yours sincerely,

JONATHAN RABAN.

PS. You can imagine the pleasure I take in the fact that I recently
had the good sense to move to the borough of Wandsworth (nice
street, lined with Alfas, BMWs and Golf GTIs, with a burglar
alarm mounted above every front door – very Club Class). My wife
and I are due to pay £148 each in Poll Tax. Eight streets away, in
Lambeth, the shiftless wastrels in the council flats are going to have
to cough up £548 a head. That'll teach them. It's all their own silly
fault, of course.

Jonathan Raban is a novelist, travel writer and critic. His books include a novel, *Foreign
Land*; three travel books, *Arabia*, *Old Glory* and *Coasting*; a personal view of London, *Soft
City*; a collection, *For Love and Money*; and *God, Man & Mrs Thatcher: a Critique of Mrs
Thatcher's Address to the Church of Scotland* (Chatto CounterBlasts, 1989).

DORIS LESSING

London NW6.

Dear Mrs Thatcher,

There is a Chinese saying which goes: 'In hard times every citizen in imagination governs the State.'
And so we are all at it.
I would like to know why a woman who has talked about good housekeeping has allowed our train services to run down to the point it is embarrassing to be in the company of people from France and Germany who take good train services for granted...why our sewage disposal services have been allowed to reach a stage where we read warnings that those water-borne diseases the Victorians defeated may be returning soon...why the far-sighted policy pursued by former governments that foreign students would be encouraged to study here by means of favourable terms has been abandoned, meaning that the special relationship this country has enjoyed with people all over the world who have thought of Britain as a second home no longer exists...why it is that one's friends in universities complain they spend their time running about trying to raise money, to the point some of them plan to emigrate...There is a good deal I would like to say. But my complaints and criticism all start from one source: that I see this Government is a mean, niggardly, short-sighted, unimaginative petty-minded administration. I wish I believed a Labour Government would be any better.

Yours sincerely,

DORIS LESSING.

Doris Lessing is a novelist and short story writer. Her many books include *The Grass is Singing*, the *Children of Violence* quintet of novels, *The Golden Notebook*, *Memoirs of a Survivor*, the five-volume *Canopus in Argus* sequence of science fiction novels, and most recently, *The Good Terrorist* and *The Fifth Child*.

COLIN WILSON

Cornwall.

Dear Mrs Thatcher,

By the time this book is published, there seems to be a fair chance that you will no longer be in office. If so, I am sure you find yourself reflecting bitterly on the short memory of the British public, and wondering how they can have proved so ungrateful – after all, it was only a year or so ago that many of them felt you were the best Prime Minister since Winston Churchill. Since I myself was one of those enthusiasts – I even wrote an admiring biographical note to your contribution to my symposium *Marx Refuted* – perhaps I may be allowed to act as spokesman for the army of defectors.

It might help if I begin by explaining how I came to be converted to the Conservative philosophy. In my mid-teens I was turned into a socialist by the arguments of Bernard Shaw. I was never a very committed leftist – having always had a deep loathing for Karl Marx and everything he stood for; still, I felt that Shaw was basically correct when he equated socialism with a 'caring society'. The socialist, said Shaw, is concerned with the general welfare of society; the capitalist is concerned only with his own profit. Therefore capitalism means selfishness and high prices; socialism means unselfishness and low prices. I must admit that I was puzzled by the fact that the price of coal had continued to rise since the mines had been nationalised; yet I was still inclined to believe that the economic philosophy of socialism is basically sound.

It was a television programme on the Japanese economic recovery that changed my mind. It pointed out that Japanese "paternalism" means that every worker feels that he is a member of a family, and that his own prosperity is intimately connected with that of his employers. He is encouraged to become a small shareholder on attractive terms, so that the prosperity of the company is reflected in his own interest statements. In short, he is also a partner in the venture.

It took precisely five minutes of watching that programme for me to cease to be a socialist. It suddenly became obvious that a man puts his best efforts into a job only when he is working for himself. If everybody's business is nobody's business, then everybody's welfare is nobody's welfare. Give a man an aim, an objective, and tell him he can achieve it by effort, and he will work at it until he drops. Tell him he is part of a group, and that everything he earns belongs by right to "society", and you destroy his mainspring of purpose.

Now at about this time, in the early 70s, I noticed an increasing feeling of anger and disillusionment in the ordinary people around me. There seemed to be a general feeling of being at the mercy of negative forces. Since the late 60s, terrorists had been hijacking aeroplanes and holding governments to ransom. The IRA had been murdering British soldiers and exploding car bombs in central Belfast. And the trade unions had no hesitation about calling strikes, no matter how great the inconvenience to the public. At about this time I was asked to give a lecture in Norway; it involved flying from London Airport in the early afternoon, to arrive at my destination about an hour before the lecture. The whole family went up to London – including three small children; we were going to snatch a brief holiday in Norway after the lecture. When we arrived at Heathrow, we were told there was a lightning strike – of baggage handlers or air traffic controllers, I have forgotten which – and we sat around in the passenger lounge until it became very clear that I was not going to get to the lecture on time. I rang the university, explained the position, and then rushed off, with three bored and disappointed children, to catch the late afternoon train back to Cornwall.

It was obvious that, with Harold Wilson as Prime Minister, no one was going to try to oppose the power of the trade unions; they were as untouchable as the Mafia, whom they resembled in so many ways. When Barbara Castle tried to do something about it, with her 'In Place of Strife' Bill, most of us knew from the beginning that it would never get off the ground – as, of course, it didn't. The trade unions promised to put their own house in order and then, of course, quietly forgot about it. And when all this came to a head in the 'Winter of Discontent', with its apparently endless series of strikes – led, of course, by the bloody-minded Ford workers – the British public had finally had enough; when it was allowed to speak its mind at the 1979 General Election, the result was the biggest national vote swing since 1945. And by Christmas, there had been an almost incredible change in the political climate. Miners had rejected a national strike call, and the British Leyland workers had voted in favour of a survival plan that involved mass redundancies. The steel workers apparently won their own dispute with a large wage settlement, but by the end of the following year, had been forced to accept massive closures. It began to look as if common sense was finally returning to British politics.

Where the economy was concerned, the next two years were grim, but I personally never had the slightest doubt that you were doing the right thing. I felt – and still feel – that you had given us back a sense of values. I didn't object in the least when anti-Thatcherites described you as schoolmistressy. Under Labour, workers had been encouraged to behave like spoilt and badly behaved children. It was marvellous to see somebody capable of knocking their heads together. It was even more wonderful, in 1982, to see you banging Argentinian heads together. When they invaded the Falklands, I expected the usual weak-willed surrender of the British government, the kind of thing that had happened at Suez in 1956. Instead, you grasped the nettle, and for the first time since the end of the war, we all had reason to feel national pride. I think no one had much doubt that, if the Labour Party had been in office, the Falklands would have remained the Malvinas for all time.

By the following year, no one had any doubt that you were on the way to a new election victory, and that you deserved it. Trade union militancy was draining away, the rate of inflation was falling, and the economy was showing signs of recovery. The last major obstacle was the miners, who had brought down the Heath Government in 1974 (largely because Heath had been ill advised enough to call a general election instead of sweating it out). Arthur Scargill was obviously the last of the union mafiosi, making thoroughly unreasonable demands – that the rest of us should pay taxes to subsidise uneconomic pits – with the certainty that his union had the brute force to impose its will. It looked at one point as if you were willing to compromise. But you dug in your heels, just as you had in the Falklands, and all the violence of the miners' pickets, and their attempts to force the steel workers to join them, ended in another victory for common sense. By 1985, I must admit that I hoped you would stay in power until the end of the century.

So what went wrong? It was not any single factor, like the Poll Tax, or the rise in interest rates brought about by Nigel Lawson's appalling blunders. Neither was it – as your opponents insisted – that your philosophy is basically "uncaring". The real problem was more subtle, and in a way more interesting. It was simply that the Tory Party, without even noticing it, began to look more and more like the old Communist Party of the Soviet Union or Romania

Decisions were handed down from above, and protests were ignored. The prescription charges have continued to rise, so that most people on an average income have to think twice before they go to the doctor. Water and electricity are to be privatised, and we all know that this means another thumping rise in prices. Everything the government does seems to be an excuse for putting a hand in our pockets. We are still paying as much for petrol as we paid at the height of the oil crisis, although the price of a barrel of oil has virtually halved – the Chancellor is grabbing the extra revenue. (I should add that the price I have to pay for a bottle of wine makes me shake my head ruefully – why are we paying so much when we are in the Common Market?) The iniquitous Unified Business Rate has already caused the closure of many factories in my part of the world – the West Country – and we hear of more every other day. But surely that is to be expected if you double or treble a business's rates?

But as far as I was concerned, the Poll Tax was certainly the last straw. I should explain immediately that I am one of the gainers – by some £200 a year – so my objection to it is not personal. Yet I was outraged by the whole idea long before the rest of the country paid any attention. The reason is simple: I can imagine how I would have felt if it had been imposed in my teens. And here some personal comment is unavoidable. I came from a working-class background and left school at sixteen. No one suggested that I should go to a university, and from the age of sixteen to twenty-four, I worked mostly in factories or in labouring jobs. I'd been determined to be a writer since I was fifteen, and served the usual apprenticeship turning out short stories, one act plays and magazine articles. Every time one of these came thumping back through the letter box – as they invariably did – the result was forty-eight hours of black depression, before I could pep-talk myself back into a state to try again. The notion of actually making a living as a writer seemed an absurd dream; but I so detested the kind of jobs I had to do to make a living that there seemed no alternative. At one point in my early twenties, I bought myself a waterproof sleeping bag, and slept out in London parks to save rent. It meant I could work for a few weeks in a factory, accumulate £20 or so, then take a month off to write my novel in the Reading Room of the British Museum. Life was pretty hard and depressing, but my luck finally turned when I began to write a book called *The Outsider* at the age of twenty-three. It appeared when I was twenty-four and made enough of a success to enable me to live by writing. I felt that

I had at last become what fate had intended me to be, a writer. But it had been an uphill struggle getting there.

Every other day I encounter young people who remind me of myself in my late teens: fairly talented, ambitious, lively, but utterly without hope about their future prospects. To tell them that they have to find £80 a year is like telling them that they have to find £8000. God knows I detest Labour and its philosophy, which seems to me a mixture of sloppy thinking and downright scoundrelism; but at least Labour governments have allowed people like these a little leeway. It seems to me an appalling lack of imagination on your part to fail to see what you are doing.

In my early twenties, I wandered into Winchester Cathedral, and came upon a pamphlet by T. S. Eliot on the uses of cathedrals in England. For the first three-quarters of the text he rambles on about the relation of cathedrals to parish churches, and I found myself wondering why he had bothered to write it. But towards the end, he speaks about the position of the dean and chapter, and the pamphlet becomes an impassioned plea for leisure in a modern society. He attacks the view that the dean and chapter should run about preaching sermons all over the parish, and argues that good theological thinking requires peace and leisure. And this was his major point: that when a society no longer has peace and leisure, when these commodities are devalued, or regarded as an excuse for laziness, then the decline of that society is inevitable.

My own basic need has always been for peace and leisure: that is why I moved to a remote part of Cornwall. You appear to believe that peace and leisure are simply another name for shirking and skiving, and – like the Communists – want to make sure that no one escapes the harness. Your economic philosophy may be the reverse of Marxism, but after ten years of Conservative government, the effect is much the same. In my teens I used to bridle at Aristotle's assertion that man is a social animal, because it seems to imply that that is *all* he is. In practice, your 'Everybody has to pay' Toryism amounts to much the same thing.

And so I am in the odd position of regarding socialist economics as feeble-minded rubbish, of groaning at the very idea that the next government might be formed by Kinnock, Hattersley and (God forbid) Gerald Kaufman, and yet of regarding another term of Thatcherism as the worst of all possible worlds. I even feel that, if Kinnock was willing to repeal the Poll Tax, it would be worth putting up with five years of socialist bungling and hot air. (I know that Chris Patten intends to "tinker" to try to make it more palatable, but it is too late; if the damage is to be undone it needs to be scrapped completely; if necessary we should return to the old rating system until something better can be devised.)

It would, of course, be impractical for you to preside over the dismantling of Poll Tax, even if you were willing to contemplate the idea. And I doubt whether it would make any difference to the electoral prospects for the Tory Party; rightly or wrongly, you are now perceived as a kind of Ceausescu, and there is an overwhelming desire throughout the country to see the back of you. Therefore, as far as I can see, the only viable alternative is for you to resign, and for your successor, whoever that is, to lose no time in announcing the start of a policy of getting rid of the Community Charge. By putting the blame on you – where, I am afraid, it squarely rests – he can escape accusations of a humiliating U-turn, and gain popular support as the saviour of the Tory Party. And provided he bears in mind that one of the main tasks of a Tory administration is to make sure that it is *never* perceived as a totalitarian government, I have no doubt that he will be Prime Minister until the mid-1990s.

I am not a particularly good political prophet. But on the last page of *Marx Refuted*, published five years ago, I foretold the downfall of European Communism within the next ten years. I confess that I did not wholly believe my own prophecy; but now that it has come about, I can see that it was inevitable. I hope that my forecast of a Labour victory at the next election will prove to be inaccurate. But I am afraid that rests entirely in your hands.

Yours etc,

Colin Wilson

COLIN WILSON.

Colin Wilson left school at 16, joined the RAF, became a tramp and worked as a labourer for several years while writing his novel *Ritual in the Dark* and his bestseller *The Outsider*, the first book of his Outsider cycle which ended with *The New Existentialism*. His formulation of a "philosophy of existence" in non-pessimistic, British terms led him to the study of many fields seemingly unrelated to philosophy: criminology, sexual deviation, the paranormal, and music.

KEN LOACH
JOHN LISTER
ALAN THORNETT

Dear Mr Kinnock,

Napoleon argued that an army marches on its stomach: but today's Labour Party is crawling on its belly. While the great commander was insisting on sustenance for his troops, you offer only peanuts to Labour supporters.

Left-wing policies have been jettisoned wholesale in the quest for a media-friendly Party image that will offend nobody. Now, after seven years of your leadership, Labour's electoral lead over the Tories depends more on gut hostility to Thatcher, and on her mistakes, than on any enthusiasm for your threadbare alternatives. Indeed hostility to the Tories has been strongest on those issues where Labour's profile has been weakest – the Miners' Strike, the ambulance dispute, the crisis of the NHS and the Poll Tax.

An electoral lead based on popular opposition to Thatcher's weaknesses – especially the crisis of an economy with inflation and interest rates – must always be vulnerable. A change in mood, a retreat on the Poll Tax, a change of Tory leader, a new racist backlash, a brief economic upturn, or more bribes from the Chancellor – any or several of these possibilities could rapidly destroy your fragile lead, losing Labour the election as well as its principles.

You are quoted as saying that 'capitalism is the system we live under, and we must make it work better': this is the heart of your politics. Yet the laws of capitalism and the market are unchanging: short-term profitability, new markets, takeovers and rationalisations will always create areas of unemployment and its attendant poverty, homelessness and deprivation. A temporary boom in Britain would export "our" recession elsewhere, and the cycle would start again. Private industry will *never* consider the long-term interests of its workers: capital always seeks out the highest rate of exploitation.

A new Labour government seems therefore doomed to repeat all the worst blunders that ensured failure for previous Labour governments. John Smith's "luncheon offensive" may be wowing the bankers and industrialists, but for workers it is as exciting as a spam sandwich. His antics confirm that your first priority is the profitability of the employers. How would you defend workers' jobs and living standards? Smith admits he wouldn't. In fact your policies are far to the right of those of Wilson or Callaghan – even committed to upholding key elements of the Tory anti-union laws, to keep organised labour "in its place".

You leave the oppressed undefended, especially those who fight back – the workers who have taken strike action; the black community of Broadwater Farm; Poll Tax protestors and non-payers; and those in the north of Ireland who suffer British army occupation. You became leader of the Party posing as a man of the left: to call you unprincipled is not abuse but a precise description of your career.

Any serious moves to eradicate exploitation and injustice must begin from precisely those socialist policies of collective ownership, workers' control and planned economy that you so vigorously reject. We need a programme which begins with measures to tackle poverty and low pay at the expense of the rich, and expand the health, welfare and education services, and which leads on to the nationalisation of private and privatised corporations, banks and finance houses. To guarantee a proper sharing of the cake, we must take over the bakery.

Instead your team tell us the Poll Tax would remain law for at least two years; that arms spending would be little changed; and that welfare spending would again have to wait in line for extra cash until the capitalist economy was "right". The very fact that Labour sees no need to confront or curb the hostile power of the mass media is testimony to your lack of any commitment to radical change.

Like a cuckoo in the nest, having ditched any "socialist" policies, you seek to oust Labour's socialists. Your courtship of the right-wing establishment has not only brought McCarthyite witch-hunting and expulsions of left-wingers, but helped drive out demoralised party activists who thought the Tories were the real enemy. Inexperienced, rootless, largely apolitical careerists are now running "new model" Labour Parties which show all the vitality of the Marie Celeste.

You protect this new status quo by pulling up the policy-making ladder behind you. While Stalinist parties in Eastern Europe embrace social democratic policies, your methods become ever more authoritarian. Your plans to cut the Party's links with the unions (to be pushed through on union block votes!), degut the reselection process, reduce the influence of active members on local parties (through postal balloting), and strip Conference of its policy-making role are all designed to insulate a Labour government from pressure from its key supporters.

These measures will increase bureaucratic centralist control over the Party, while killing its local organisations and jeopardising its roots in the working class. Far from moving forward into the 1990s, these changes take the Party back to the pre-1906 era, in which the political horizons of the working class were limited to the fringes of the Liberal Party.

However hard you may try to drive out the class struggle, it will always return. Since last summer we have seen a revival of trade union struggles and Poll Tax protests galvanising thousands of young workers against the Tories. Reports that the working class was dead were greatly exaggerated.

The more successfully you break the Labour Party from the working class movement and transform it into a purely parliamentary, top-down electoral machine like the US Democrats, the more you will replicate the political pressures that led to the formation of the Labour Party itself in its break from the Liberals. You are now the most powerful factor promoting a renewed round of political struggles or even splits in the workers' movement.

You may look with disdain on those that hold loyal to socialist politics, and who are organising minority forces in the unions and Labour Party in opposition to your policies, but the history books will not prize your Canute-style efforts to hold back the class struggle and channel it into the backwater of "new realism". The working class, unbroken by eleven years of Thatcherism, will not be satisfied or long forestalled by the policies you are offering: it can only find its goal in socialism.

Yours fraternally,

Ken Loach.   *John Lister*   *Alan Thornett*

KEN LOACH
JOHN LISTER
ALAN THORNETT.

Ken Loach is a television and film director. His films and documentaries include *Cathy Come Home, Up the Junction, Days of Hope, Kes, Family Life, Looks and Smiles* and *Hidden Agenda*. John Lister is a freelance journalist. Alan Thornett is a trades unionist, formerly TGWU deputy convenor at British Leyland's Cowley plant.

ARNOLD WESKER

London N19,
6 September 1989.

Dear Neil,

It seems as though we can't get together for quite some time. October the thinking is. Let me therefore put down some of the thoughts I would have put to you as someone who, though he's never been a member of the Labour Party, or any party, would like to see you become the next Prime Minister.

I offer them with some trepidation and *not* as a student of politics or as a Kinnock-watcher – I'm afraid it takes me all my time to watch the clock to earn my living as a writer. I read the press and follow what I can on TV. What I mean is I'm no expert in anything other than my own plays and it may be that I'm putting to you what has been either considered and dismissed or done and I'm unaware of it.

I'm prompted to these thoughts because of one of the last things you flung in my direction as we left the restaurant those weeks ago. You were asking how can the Left regain authority over the issues around individual liberty. How can the initiative be wrested from Thatcher? I think the answer lies in your personality. What follows are thoughts to do with you, not with Labour manifestos and policy. Except obliquely.

What we need is to know you, the man as thinker. There exist fundamental themes which philosophers and writers, among others, have wrestled with since Adam.

Which are they and what do you think about them? They need to be identified. For each of us the themes are different. What does your set consist of ? Humankind's irrationality? The cycle between injustice – revolution – injustice – revolution? The chimera of utopia? The nature of good and evil?

It would be an event of paramount importance if you were to give something like the Reith Lectures. I don't know if they have a format requiring the lecturer to address the problems of communication. My memory is that they can be wide-ranging. But if not the Reith Lectures then a lecture tour to no more than six venues where it would be known that you were going to address a major theme every three months leading up to the general election.

The Kinnock Lectures: Six Milestones to Election Day

Examples: 'The Individual Spirit'. Does a capitalist society really
shackle or free it? The image of capitalism which D. H. Lawrence
presented of 400 donkeys running after the carrot which only one
can get still remains imaginatively impressive for me. On the other
hand there is no doubt that a free market seems to release
individual imagination and initiative. And the socialist parties of the
West have suffered because of the suppression, up till recently, of
the individual spirit in Eastern Bloc "socialist" countries. It would
be important to hear you on this theme of 'the free spirit'. As an
artist I believe profoundly in the free spirit. It is what most of my
writing is about. Of course I believe in the need for social
responsibility as well but I believe one should be free to engage or
not in such responsibility. The only freedom not permissible is
freedom to be anti-social. I touch upon the theme at its simplest
level. The point is: what does the man who may become the next
Prime Minister of the United Kingdom think?

'Political priorities'. What are yours? The answer should not be a
long list which one could find in the party manifesto, but more a
philosophical answer. I am no philosopher or political thinker but if
I were asked the question on, say, *Any Questions* I think I would like
to explore two: liberty and education. Not 'the economy'. I'd like to
hear a political leader say the economy of a nation is *not* a central
consideration. Yes, important, of course, but oh to hear a politician
say: 'economics is to do with house-keeping. Every family knows
how important it is to house-keep wisely *but life is not about house-
keeping*'. Maggie captured the imagination of an unexpectedly vast
number of working-class supporters because she appealed to 'the
common sense of the house-wife...who knows you cannot spend
what you haven't earned'. Well, apart from the fact that it was
economic nonsense since banking exists to lend people money they
haven't earned in the hope they will spend it in order to earn more,
the other response is: but are we only to be addressed as house-
keepers? Do we see our people as nothing more? Is keeping house
the limit of human aspiration? House-keeping is the least we expect
of government – and no government has ever *really* got it right
anyway, has it? It's like saying the most important part of the
furniture-maker's skill is his ability to use his chisel. But that's the
least one expects a furniture-maker to be able to do. It's the chair
that's important. After all he may use his chisel expertly to make the
most ugly and uncomfortable chair imaginable.

Yes, I know your opponents would have a field-day with the man who would be Prime Minister saying the economy is not the priority. But getting the economy right is like preparing the soil. Get the mixture right, drain it well, keep an eye on it, but what are you going to encourage to grow there.

Perhaps saying it is not a central consideration is to invite red-herrings. I'll re-phrase it: the economy is so primary that the weight of our attention must inevitably be upon it; so much so that it's foolish to go on about it, like claiming a virtue out of a necessity. It's the very first thing a government must do. Big deal! But a penny off tax here, a rise of ten pounds there is not the be and end of it all. Economic security is one route to freedom but education is just as important a route.

From the themes of liberty and education come sub-themes. Crime, for example. It seems to me that the nature of crime is essentially fascist in that it curtails freedom. We and our children cannot walk the streets at night. I would double the police force and ensure every police officer had a liberal education as well as learnt how to fire a gun. A strong – but enlightened – police-force is central to a free society. That's an apparent paradox needing to be explored.

'Language and political inhumanity', is the theme of an important essay by George Steiner who paralleled the rise of Nazism with the decline of the usage of the German language. What do you feel about political language? Political rhetoric? Why does there exist a great scepticism of the way politicians speak? How much do you care about the words you use, how much do you think about nuance, distinctions, metaphor? As a politician you have to debate and you have to address the nation and you have to employ words to shape the reasoning behind your decisions. What do you have to say about language that will lead voters to trust you?

'Violence and terrorism – self-defeating'. What thoughts have you about the international scene so dominated by violent actions? Where has this violence sprung from? Is there such an emotion as the 'politics of envy'? What does it mean? Perhaps the envy should be acknowledged, addressed head-on. If Gorbachev will be remembered as a great statesman it will as much for his ability to say they made mistakes as for his contribution to reducing East-West military tensions. Perhaps someone in the West should acknowledge the colonial past and say but we cannot go on holding each other responsible for what our grandfathers did. Or perhaps someone has to say: look! the truth is I don't like you. Your values

and systems appal me, but! we don't *have* to love each other! we just
somehow have to live together, reach a *modus vivendi*. You who are
taking hostages, planting bombs on planes, living secret lives of
revenge, you too have become your own victims because you cannot
live normal or fulfilled lives.

'The world a global village'. How would you use technology?
Would you have a voting button in every house which can be
pushed to give you an idea of how the nation felt about an
important decision you had to make? I read recently that the first
international court case was proceeding by satellite. Would you use
satellite to host a television meeting, a confrontation, between
world leaders, say four times a year, in which for a two-hour period
(no 30 minute rushed exchanges) you would raise and debate a
major issue troubling those leaders at that moment?

Which touches on another theme – the functioning of governments in the future. How open do you believe government should
be? I personally want to see Parliament on TV, the show-offs can
be seen through and will soon become discredited. But more – I
would like to see the world's leaders ask each other awkward
questions in public, and press and press until a kind of truth is
wrung ot them. I want to hear what you think of the exercise of
politics in an age of incredible technology.

A banker once said to me – he had just returned from helping
the French Government get back to privatisation from nationalisation – that it was not the purpose of government to run businesses.
Well, maybe yes and maybe no. The purpose of government, it
seems to me, is the old one of creating a framework within which
the life of its citizens can be lived with the greatest degree of
fulfilment and happiness. If that involves creating government
enterprises – like transport and the health service then that is
fulfilling its function; if it involves leaving the banks and insurance
and the docks to private enterprise, then that is fulfilling the
function. If citizens need to be protected from the tyranny of
private monopolies or trade unions then that is fulfilling the
function of government. Dogma is the death of all things. So it
seems to me. But what do you feel about the nature of government?

Can you see what I'm looking for? I have identified themes which
preoccupy me, but they may not preoccupy you. What we want to
know is what themes *do* preoccupy you. And they should be
delivered on mixed occasions: a union conference, the George
Orwell Lecture at Birkbeck, the Raymond Williams Memorial
Lecture in the Hay on Wye Festival of Literature...As a dramatist

I'd like to see a series of addresses which build and build to a
climax. Each conclusion should lead on to the theme of the next
lecture. And they should not be cosy thoughts, they should be
controversial...Kinnock on morality, on culture (the arts), on
nationalism, on bureaucracy and corruption, on our grandfather's
sins, on the power of words and the responsibility involved...

Gorbachev has captured imaginations by, in a way, being
unpredictable, unexpected. He has not behaved as we have come to
expect a politician to behave. There is something cheeky and fresh
about him. We are all tired of stale politicians, and their stale,
careful ways. We want to know the thinking behind the thought.
We want to experience an event that will reveal Neil Kinnock the
thinker, and that will have the nation humming and talking and
arguing and writing letters to *The Times*, about what Kinnock has
said on the theme of this, that and the other, because the thought,
the language, the imagery were memorable, quotable, vivid, witty,
startling.

We are not looking for the gimmick, not something attention-
grabbing for attention-grabbing's sake, and certainly not for yet
another political speech. But for that which will fix you in the
imagination of the public, which suddenly makes all of us, even the
cynical pressfolk, sit up and say hey! we've been called upon to
think new thoughts and dance! Kennedy, whatever else his faults,
opened the White House to artists. Gorbachev introduced two new
words to the international dictionary. De Gaulle took France out of
Algeria. Sadat went to Jerusalem...

Is all that I've written presumptious, foolish, not within the
province of the political leader? Perhaps the majority of British
voters don't want a thinking politician. The intellectual has always
been suspect in this country.

Consider it or reject it, but do so in the spirit with which it is
offered – concern. And let's talk over Dusty's dinner table with a
couple of other writers if you still feel you'd like to.

. . . .

30 October 1989

Dear Neil,

It worries me hugely that you have my last letter hanging over your
head. Please don't think about responding to it. You have far more
important considerations. You've read it. If anything I've said gels,

fine. You are surrounded by far more authoritative advisers. I almost regret my presumption.

Nevertheless I'll throw one last comment in before I fly off to Oslo where, as I think I told you, I'm directing *The Merry Wives of Windsor*. Beware of the phrase that strains too hard. I heard you describe Nicholas Ridley's successor as 'the slick following the nick'. Later I heard you describe Maggie's policy on entering the European monetary system as 'the politics of Garbo – leave me alone, I want to be alone'. Whoever put those to you – sack them! The Garbo image misfires. The one who goes it alone is often the most attractive, the hero who is out of step with the mad times, the individualist who stands up against mob hysteria. Remember *Twelve Angry Men* – Henry Fonda stood out against all the other members of the jury and made them doubt their verdict of guilty.

Maggie is impressive. I saw her interviewed by Walden last night. She was also lucky, he asked her all the questions she's used to answering. No one really challenges her on the reality of her dogmas. No one, for example, puts it to her that the state's duty could be to protect the individual from the tyrannical control of industrial thugs. We're living in an age of Thatcher's Thugs, in fact.

Anyway, I've written more than I intended. My wish was to relieve you, not burden you further. Writers! Show them a blank page and they *have* to fill it!

Kind regards,

[signature]

ARNOLD WESKER.

Arnold Wesker is the author of 30 plays which include *Roots*, *Chips With Everything*, *Love Letters on Blue Paper*, *Shylock* and *When God Wanted a Son*, and of three volumes of short stories and two collections of essays. His collected plays are published in six volumes by Penguin Books. He has just written the libretto for an opera of his play *Caritas*, for music by Robert Saxton, commissioned by Opera North.

Neil Kinnock attended a performance of *Roots* at the National Theatre in 1989, and dined with Wesker afterwards. In these two letters Wesker elaborates various points raised during their discussions.

Michael Winner is a film director, producer and writer, best known for his *Death Wish* series of films. He has led all-industry campaigns against restrictive censorship. He is a senior Council member of the Directors Guild of Great Britain and a Trustee of the London Hospital Children's Ward Appeal, and founder and Chairman of the Police Memorial Trust, which erects roadside memorials to slain police officers.

MICHAEL WINNER

London W8.

Dear Mrs Thatcher,

May I deal with important matters first. You really must serve better canapés at Number 10. They do not signify you are in the presence of one of the great leaders of an important nation. I do not, myself, drink (although my friends were a little scathing about the alcohol as well!) but there is a noticeable lack of ice for those of us leading by example and taking soft drinks.

While I remember, could you please tell dear Mr Kinnock not to shout so much when he makes his speeches both in the House of Commons and before his assembled multitudes throughout the land. Could you impress upon him that in these days of high technology such as microphones and loudspeakers he does not have to behave as if the only way he can be heard at the back of the hall is to make a great deal of noise.

I have noticed a considerable improvement in your own delivery since you first took office but if you need a few tips on how to make it even more becoming you can always give me a call.

It would be nice if you could redouble your efforts to help the British film industry. I know they largely make films about socialists in South London or somnambulant people in Wales in the early 1900s, but we're awfully nice people. I wonder if you could instil in the film community here a belief that to make a popular film is not necessarily an unfortunate vulgarity.

After all, you don't expect the National Theatre, the Shakespeare Theatre or the Royal Opera House to show a profit and whilst we may have carried loss-making to extremes, you must admit that from time to time our films wave the flag rather well.

You've done awfully well in cutting down the number of old Etonians in the Cabinet although some of the people you've replaced them with are a little odd, don't you think?

We need a bit of a shake-up in our educational system which still seems to produce a load of toffee-nosed twits at the top who rush into the City and get up to all sorts of dubious practices and a load of embittered layabouts who inhabit the lower end. Why don't we chuck half the pupils out of our public schools (over half of them are useless anyway!) and fill their places with livelier minds from the so-called lower classes and ethnic minorities? Then they can all be educated together initially in conflict but doubtless at the end in great harmony and learn a bit about each other in the process.

I suggest you instigate next year as 'Building Removal Year'. You have permitted those dreadful property speculators to add grossly to the number of grotesquely dull, tedious office and apartment blocks. I think the unemployed should be paid to attack them, pack them up in little plastic bags and dump them somewhere (preferably not near me) and then plant trees and gardens in their place.

I could suggest a few good starting points around me where the most beautiful Victorian buildings have been removed to be replaced by quite horrible structures which are in need of instant demolition.

I think it's wonderful the way you persuaded Mr Gorbachev to pack in all that Communist nonsense and adopt a jolly capitalist society instead. Next time you speak to him could you ask him to let me have a monthly delivery of twenty-five 100 gram tins of fresh Beluga caviar and do be sure to tell him I prefer the tins to the glass jars because they do better in the fridge.

We must do something to get you better appreciated by that nice American, Mr Bush. It seems so unfair that while you and Ronnie were so close he should not show you the same warmth and humanity. Perhaps Denis could be our Ambassador in Washington. It would jolly things up no end.

I can think of a few more requests, but I don't want to appear selfish.

My kindest personal regards.

Yours sincerely,

MICHAEL WINNER.

PS. Do give my best to Michael Heseltine if you ever talk to him. He does have far and away the best hair of anyone in the Conservative Party and that alone should be enough to secure him in his position as your successor, don't you think?

PETER BARNES

London W2.

Dear Mr Kinnock,

Surprise me.

We live in one of the most callous societies in Western Europe with leaders who have the compassion and ethics of a pack of starving jackals; a popular press which is an open sewer owned by men of obscene wealth befouling everything it touches; a spineless, irrelevant Church; a ludicrous, class-ridden judiciary; a neglected Health Service; an unjust education system and a police force which is no better than the criminals it fails to catch. Surprise me and change it if you get the chance.

I have no great hopes only fears for if I hear the truth spoken by politicians, I immediately assume they are doing it only because they have no inducement to lie. I also know how difficult it is to change anything in this country, having spent all my writing life trying to help create a people who are sceptical, rational, critical, not easily fooled or impressed. In a word a free people – ungovernable. It is a mad dream of course especially given that the English are forever deferential to those above them whilst despising those below them, passionate only in their protection of the miserable "status quo". Why do they do it? Why did Dorothy want to go back to Kansas where everything was black and white?

For my part I am against those who give orders. This does not mean I reject all authority. I just try to keep my hat on in its presence. In the matter of bread we talk to a baker, in the matter of plumbing a plumber, a house, a builder. For special knowledge we apply to a specialist. But we don't allow the baker, plumber or builder to impose their authority over us. We listen to them with the respect they merit – if any – but we retain our right to judge and criticise. There is no reason to treat elected or non-elected leaders any different. Always look at the bill, we have to pay it.

Surprise me, and see that Socialism is something you can't find anywhere in the world but there is nevertheless a place where you can find it: it is not a certainty but a value. Surprise me and agree its aim is simply to make people happier and less oppressed; to promote a socially just society. For no clever theories can get round the fact that the rich live by robbing the poor who get nothing much in return but ugly lives. The sad fact is that the majority of humanity is worse off today than it was in the 15th century; worse because our poverty is deliberately imposed by the strong and does not spring from a catastrophe of nature.

The Conservative Party's purpose is to defend the existence of such inequalities. In the last ten years we have gone through the Passion in reverse, for in the Passion one man suffered for everybody, here everybody suffered for one woman. Surprise me and try to bring about a resurrection.

I have little hope, given the Labour Party's weasel-eyed, jelly-spined, Charlotterusse response to the attack on a fellow writer, Salman Rushdie, by Allah's bearded book-burners.

Surprise me. Ignore hard-headed advisors, commentators and experts who whisper of "real politik" and making "tough decisions" – it is curious how tough decisions are always tough on others, never on the people advocating toughness. Goodness is not weakness but a positive, manly virtue. There is no better epitaph than 'He was a good man who did good things'. Perhaps that is asking too much. In the end it will be enough if they can say 'He acted justly, loved mercy and never trumped his partner's ace'.

Surprise me.

If you would like to meet, ring me and I will give you my phone number.

Yours sincerely,

Peter Barnes

PETER BARNES.

Peter Barnes is a dramatist and theatre director. His plays are collected in *Plays: One* (Methuen): these include *The Ruling Class* and *Red Noses*. He has won the John Whiting Award, Evening Standard Award, Giles Cooper Radio Award, and the Laurence Olivier Award for best play of the year, and the Royal Television Society Award for the best television drama of the year.

BLOODAXE BOOKS

Winner of the Sunday Times Small Publishers' Award 1990

'Bloodaxe Books has established a ferocious reputation as a publisher of ground-breaking modern poetry. It has cornered a market in the publishing industry with flair, imagination and conspicuous success' – SUNDAY TIMES.

Bloodaxe Books is an international literary publishing house based in Newcastle. As well as publishing famous names in literature from all over the world, Bloodaxe has discovered and helped establish the reputations of many of Britain's most promising new writers, and now publishes more new poetry books than any other British publisher. Its list also includes modern fiction, politics, photography, drama, biography and literary criticism.

SELECTED TITLES

SEEDS OF FIRE, *edited by Geremie Barmé & John Minford*
'The best understanding of the sources of China's deep malaise comes from a worm's eye view. *Seeds of Fire* is an anthology of Chinese protest literature. It is an outstanding collection of short stories, poems, prose, excerpts from novels, plays, sketches, songs, interviews, declarations, manifestos – the lot – concerned with *la condition humaine chinoise* in the 20th century ' – CYRIL LIN, *New Statesman*. 'Required reading for anyone interested in contemporary China' – GRAHAM THOMAS, *Times Educational Supplement*. 544 pages: £7.95 paper.

IRINA RATUSHINSKAYA: *No, I'm Not Afraid*
Why was a 28-year-old woman sentenced to seven years' hard labour for writing these poems? Second edition of the book which spearheaded an international campaign which secured the author's release in 1986. Translated by David McDuff, with documentary material supplied by Amnesty International. 144 pages: £5.95 paper & £12.95 cloth.

IRINA RATUSHINSKAYA: *Pencil Letter*
Poems written in the women's labour camp where Irina was imprisoned for four years. Translated by Alan Myers, Carol Rumens, David McDuff, Richard McKane and others. 96 pages: £4.95 paper & £10.95 cloth.

TONY HARRISON: *v.*
The controversial poem filmed by Channel Four which made front page headlines in the tabloids. 'This work of singular nastiness' – MARY WHITEHOUSE. 'The criticism against the poem has been offensive, juvenile and, of course, philistine' – HAROLD PINTER. As well as the poem itself, this second edition includes photographs, press articles, letters, reviews, a defence

of the poem and film by director Richard Eyre, and a transcript of the phone
calls logged by Channel Four on the night of the broadcast.
80 pages: £4.95 paper.

TOM PAULIN: *Ireland & the English Crisis*
Outspoken essays on Irish and English literature and culture, including
Paulin's famous polemic against Conor Cruise O'Brien, attacks on structural-
ists, and important accounts of Joyce, Lawrence and Ian Paisley.
224 pages: £7.95 paper.

HINTERLAND, *edited by E. A. Markham*
Substantial selections, with interviews and essays by the poets on their work,
make this anthology the definitive textbook of Caribbean poetry from the West
Indies and Britain. 'E. A. Markham's anthology of Caribbean poetry in English
should be ordered at once by all those who go by the title of Head of English' –
CAROL ANN DUFFY, *Guardian*. 336 pages: £7.95 paper & £16 cloth.

POETRY WITH AN EDGE, *edited by Neil Astley*
The best of Bloodaxe: a startling anthology of work by over 50 British, Irish,
American and European poets celebrating ten years of Bloodaxe Books. 'As an
introduction to the best contemporary poetry, this anthology is invaluable' –
PETER SIRR, *Irish Times*. 'This is a vital and catholic anthology, one of the best,
in terms of value for money, since *The Rattle Bag*' – DAVID PROFUMO, *Sunday
Times*. 320 pages: £7.95 paper.

MIROSLAV HOLUB: *Poems Before & After*
Collected English translations of Czechoslovakia's most important poet. 'One
of the half dozen most important poets writing anywhere' – TED HUGHES.
'One of the sanest voices of our time' – A. ALVAREZ. 'A magnificent volume' –
TOM PAULIN, *Independent on Sunday*. 'These poems are the fruit of Holub's
convictions. If his work is representative of anything beyond its own startling
originality, it should be seen as embodying the authentic spirit of European
humanism, with its traditions of learning and unfettered intellectual enquiry.
He is a writer of immense importance and accomplishment' – NEW
STATESMAN. 276 pages: £7.95 paper & £16 cloth.

MARIN SORESCU: *The Biggest Egg in the World*
New poems by Romania's comic genius in versions by Ted Hughes, Seamus
Heaney, David Constantine, D. J. Enright, Michael Hamburger, Michael
Longley, Paul Muldoon and William Scammell, co-translated with Ioana
Russell-Gebbett. 80 pages: £4.95 paper.

SIMON ARMITAGE: *Zoom!*
'Astonishingly good for such a young writer...poems with an energy which
comes directly from life now and the living language' – CAROL ANN DUFFY,
Guardian. Poetry Book Society Choice, shortlisted for the Whitbread Prize.
80 pages: £5.95 paper.

For a complete catalogue of Bloodaxe titles, please write to:
Bloodaxe Books Ltd, P.O. Box 1SN, Newcastle upon Tyne NE99 1SN.